CW00662446

Roses on the Terrace at Dalemain rambling over the ancient walls above the Low Garden.

BETWEEN TWO GARDENS

The Diary of two Border gardens

by

Sylvia Mary McCosh

DALEMAIN   PENRITH   CUMBRIA
HUNTFIELD   BIGGAR   SCOTLAND

© Sylvia Mary McCosh 1982

ISBN 0 900811 17 X

Printed and distributed by Titus Wilson & Son Ltd.
28 Highgate, Kendal, Cumbria

ACKNOWLEDGEMENTS

My thanks are due to Mrs. Pat Dunbar for all the trouble she has taken in typing my manuscripts and to Tom Wright for the photographs on the cover and facing page 58.

Dedicated to Bryce
to whom both Dalemain and
I owe so much

Our England is a garden, and such gardens are not made
By singing: "Oh how beautiful!" and sitting in the shade . . . .
Rudyard Kipling

FOREWORD

Having at various times in my life seen most of the best gardens in Great Britain, I am more than ever convinced that the most interesting ones are those, small enough to reflect the owner's taste and personality. For many of us even one garden can prove too much as we grow older and suffer from physical and financial difficulties, but here we read of an author whose unbounded energy and enthusiasm runs two gardens comfortably some ninety-six miles apart, with very little help.

Each has its own attraction, and each is full of good plants and always colourful. I hope that those who read this book, will catch some of the enthusiasm and be tempted to try different plants. Anything which grows at Dalemain or Huntfield must be extremely hardy, as neither can be said to have a good climate, though the beauty of the surroundings makes up for a good deal.

Recently I was honoured by being asked to make the speech at the party to celebrate the family being at Dalemain for three hundred years. One wonders what gardens will be like in another three hundred years, but one thing of which I am certain is that Dalemain will still be lovely and I hope, able to continue to give so much pleasure to those who visit its beauty.

Crossrigg Hall   *Cornish Torbock*

For the flowers are great blessings,
For the Lord made a Nosegay in the medow with his
   disciples and preached upon the lily.
For the angels of God took it out of his hand and
   carried it to the Height . . .
For there is no Height in which there are not flowers.
For flowers have great virtues for all the senses.
For the flower glorifies God and the root parries the
   adversary.
For the flowers have their angels even the words of
   God's Creation.
For the warp and woof of flowers are worked by
   perpetual moving spirits.
For flowers are good both for the living and the dead.
For there is a language of flowers.
For there is a sound reasoning upon all flowers.
For elegant phrases are nothing but flowers.
For flowers are peculiarly the poetry of Christ.
For flowers are medicinal.
For flowers are musical in ocular harmony.
For the right names of flowers are yet in heaven,
   God make gardeners better nomenclators.
For the Poorman's nosegay is an introduction to a
   Prince . . . .
                    Christopher Smart 1722-71

PROLOGUE

The Story of Two Gardens

This is the diary for our two gardens for the Year of our Lord 1980. Firstly, for the garden at Dalemain, the much loved home of my family who have lived there for over three hundred years. This ancient house, gathered together through the centuries, was built at a strategic point among the meadowlands near to a place where the Dacre Beck tumbles into the larger river Eamont, whose quiet waters flow peacefully among fields and woody places. Just out of sight, and beyond the undulating parkland, the great lake of Ullswater lies in a deep valley, winding its way like a ribbon of ever changing colours between the mighty fells where the sun and the wind chase one another according to their fancies.

I was born in the nursery at Dalemain in time for breakfast one November morning. Children have played and slept in these nurseries for many generations, and here Nanny ruled in her little kingdom where a good fire burned cosily all the year round; the shining, black-leaded grate was well protected by a heavy guard whose shining brass top rail aired the little garments we children wore.

The nursery opened on to the broad white scrubbed stair-case, once the new front stairs in the seventeenth century; they were very convenient for little feet to reach the outside world, and for nursery meals to be carried up from the kitchen on heavy wooden trays. Beyond the low windows in the nursery lay the cobbled courtyard, the great barn, the stables and a host of farm buildings. Standing on one of the low window seats I was soon able to watch all that was going on outside, and to listen to the low moo-ing of the cows and calves housed warmly beneath the huge loft, where quantities of sweet smelling hay were stored away every summer. The constant sound of horses' hooves made merry music; the hunting horses constantly being led in or out of the red stable doors across the courtyard, or Dick the trap horse being shined and polished while he stood obediently tied to a ring in the stable wall, before being yoked to the dog cart, which then swayed drunkenly across the cobbles and the puddles as he was driven to Penrith to collect parcels, or to the station to pick up a passenger. Heavy-footed Clydesdale farm horses were led across the yard for their early morning drink from rain-water barrels before they were fed; later they were hitched into carts with much clanking and rattling of chains. The courtyard was never dull for a moment; people came and went; carpets and blankets were shaken on "the green" on fine days; rabbits and game were carried in or out of the huge game safes that were perched on stilts underneath a group of sycamore trees that grew not far from the back door.

Across "the green", where ducks and hens waddled their way in search of food and grubs, and safely hidden behind enormously high walls, lay the gardens; snapdragons seeded themselves like wild flowers in the crevices of the stone and covered these walls with a multitude of colour all through the summer months. The beautiful rambling gardens which had grown up with the centuries, were my playground, where I learned to sow seeds and plant pansies and all the little flowers that children love to grow; I always loved to grow plants and to feel the kindly soil running through my fingers; wild flowers there were in plenty too, some rare, and many exquisite beauties growing profusely in our wonderful little corner of Britain. To search for wild flowers and to record them in our nature note books was one of the chief activities of schoolroom life when Etta Murray became governess to my sister and myself. I was nine years old and Margaret was six. Etta's father was a yeoman farmer and her mother was one of the first District Nurses, whose only means of transport in those days was on a bicycle or perhaps a hurried journey in a pony cart.

We lived a country life and learnt of country matters. It was from this home, that meant so much to me, that Bryce and I were married in 1948, soon after the holocaust of the second world war had ended.

Bryce's home was an old white house called Hardington which was built on a bank above tree-lined parks close to the great river Clyde. Comfortable heather-covered hills rambled on all sides with Tinto, the Hill of Fire, standing as a lonely landmark on the edge of Thankerton moor, with the Douglas moors beyond the hill called Dungavel sweeping up to the skies above the little hamlet of Wiston. On these hills Bryce and his many cousins played as children and shot the wild grouse which fed on the flowers of the heather. Those heartbreaking war-time years had taken him far away sailing the high seas with the Wavy Navy, but when peace came and the world was settling down in its aftermath, we met at a party in a friend's house not far from Hardington; those same beautiful hills which we both love so much, seemed to bring us together.

*   *   *

The diary is also for Huntfield, our comfortable Scottish home hidden away among those same high heathery hills and quiet woodlands on the borders of the counties of Lanark and Peebles. The avenue leading up to the house is overhung with interweaving branches of maples, beeches, and horse-chestnuts, and when the evening sunbeams shine their long gold fingers down the drive through the arching branches, one has the illusion of driving through some wondrous cathedral.

Huntfield had been a small independent estate for a very long time, when the surrounding lands of Shieldhill had belonged to the Chancellor family, and previously to the powerful Somerville family who came to Scotland with the Norman conquerors. Huntfield was just the sort of home we had dreamed of, with a fertile farm that stretched along the low side of the heather-covered hills where we could graze ponies and Blackfaced sheep. The earliest date we can find above a doorway is 1796, but in the early nineteenth century the owners were a family called Stark who were closely associated with the building of Edinburgh Royal Infirmary and other works of enlightenment which were taking place during the reign of Queen Victoria. It was one of the Stark family who planted many trees at Huntfield and introduced some of the rarer varieties which were being discovered by plant explorers in the lands across the seas in those days of great enterprise.

The lands around the house were thickly wooded, including the hills above the house. In 1879 a terrible storm swept the countryside; it was the night of the long remembered Tay Bridge disaster when the Edinburgh to Inverness train was lost as the bridge collapsed in the teeth of the gale. Further south trees were piteously uprooted, including the great wood on Huntfield Hill, which was blown flat. It took ten years to clear the fallen timber, which was laboriously carted the three miles to Thankerton railway station by Clydesdale horses. The hill was never replanted, and except for a few remaining trees which serve as convenient posting points for cuckoos in the early summer, the ground was soon covered once more by heather, grasses and wild flowers.

Soon after the end of the Great War, the estate was purchased in 1919 by Miss Ellen Dunlop, an astute elderly lady of the late Victorian era whose father had bought the Shieldhill estate at the turn of the century. Her mother died when she was born, and as she grew up she looked after her father and ran the house, and later turned Huntfield, which she had bought as a more suitably sized house for her old age, into a home for the children of widowers; they were children of all ages mainly from the Glasgow area. There were always two or three babies among them so that they could be brought up as a big family. It was a happy house, and the children had a world of their own outside in which to play. They could dam the burns that mysteriously appear from the hundreds of little springs on the hillsides, or play in the woods and make little gardens, and they went to school in Biggar with all the other children from round about. From time to time they went back to Glasgow for holidays with their fathers, if their father could manage to look after them, but they always came back to Huntfield. Even to this day grown-up people return to see the house where they grew up and which they learnt to love as "home".

Besides the children, two ladies *"of small means"* came for holidays, all through the summer days, and when they went away another two arrived to take their place.

When the war ended, Miss Dunlop and her companion Jeannie Macdonald moved up to Huntfield. Ellen's father was dead and Shieldhill was sold back to the Chancellor family. Jeannie Macdonald was a wonderful person; her father had been the coachman and she started her working life as a schoolroom maid to the motherless girl, and they became life-long friends. Jeannie's family came from Skye, but, though her school days must have been short, she was able to cope with all Miss Dunlop's affairs, including her income tax returns.

When we bought Huntfield and moved in with our three boys, ponies, dogs, and our old white cat "Winnie Pooh-Pooh", Jeannie became a real friend to us all. Miss Dunlop, having no close relations, hoped that Huntfield would become a real family home; and so it was. Robert and Andy slept in the cosiest bedroom in the house which had been the night nursery for the motherless children, while Ted chose a room at the top of the house which had a marvellous view across the hill, and from which he could watch his poultry – bantams, ducks, and turkeys, guinea fowl and the rest. Nanny took up residence in the sunniest room which we chose to be the nursery, where Peter Rabbit and his friends ran perpetually round the wall frieze. When she came to us as Nanny to our children, her old-fashioned trunk came too, and we felt that she had come to stay. Ted was six months old, and as the years passed our halos widened. Jeannie Macdonald was left a cosy house and land too, in the tiny village of Quothquan. She always came to tea with us on Christmas Day and on many other occasions: we went to see her frequently; sometimes we drove along the quiet road to see her in the pony trap, and the sight always filled her with joy, reminding her of happy days of long ago.

We have lived at Huntfield for twenty-three years, and it is there that our three boys have really grown up, although they were all born in Ayrshire, where we lived for ten previous years. During those years we lived at Brownhill, a dear, white-washed house, perched on the hillside above the Garnock Valley. We made our first "proper" garden there, although we made valiant attempts to create gardens in our two earlier homes in which we lived soon after the end of the war when it was extremely difficult for "newly marrieds" to find a house, let alone one with a little garden.

Brownhill, in the soft Ayrshire climate, produced all manner of plants: roses grew with no trouble; primulas, herbaceous plants and vegetables. Huge old yew trees spread their great branches to form archways between the small walled orchard and the shady lawn in front of the house: they made an imposing spectacle as one drove down the avenue to the red front door. A group of buddleias growing near the house taught me that it was necessary to prune them back very hard every February in order to produce an abundance of flowers and to prevent them being blown to pieces in the wind. There I learnt to prune fruit trees, which repaid every effort, for we could see the red apples glowing in the sunlight from our bedroom windows. I bought a little book entitled "Simple Pruning" and read it from cover to cover.

It was heartbreaking to leave Brownhill where we had all been so happy; where the children had played make-believe, and made houses for their invisible friends. Andy was only eighteen months old when we moved, but by that time he was running about in tiny red wellington boots with a big basket which he filled with "useful" things.

When we moved to Lanarkshire, half the garden moved too. We had collected lovely old stone troughs of all shapes and sizes from a stone-mason nearby, and it needed a cattle float to move them and all our possessions, quite apart from the furniture.

One of the treasures we found at Brownhill was a shell-pink shrub rose which has not been identified as yet, but may be one of Chinese rose origin. It has semi-double flowers with beautiful stamens, dark-coloured young growth, shiny leaves, and grows about eight feet tall; in the early summer it is a mass of somewhat floppy, tea-rose type of flowers. Fortunately it was reasonably easy to propagate,, and a bundle of cuttings moved with us which have since grown into notable bushes.

Eighteen months after leaving Ayrshire we found Huntfield, a comfortable, partly eighteenth century and partly Victorian house, not too big, but large enough to have two staircases. Twenty years on, we were able to divide the house when Andy, the first of our boys to be married, was anxious to move from Edinburgh back to the country. He and Sue took over the "South Wing" which contained the older turned stair-case, and in due course when David and Saya were born, the house and our lives were filled with happiness. How Miss Dunlop must have rejoiced with us to see Huntfield so fully occupied; she had been a generous benefactor to the neighbourhood, a pillar of the Kirk and president of Quothquan Women's Rural Institutes, the second branch to be started of this great organisation in Scotland. She and Jeannie Macdonald used to walk on the hills with lanterns in moonlight evenings, when the moon and the stars chased each other in and out of the clouds, as they still do. Since they always fed the birds, she left a sum of money in her will so that they might be fed, as in her day. Not a tree was allowed to be cut, and there were some magnificent trees near the garden, including two Wellingtonias, a Himalayan Cedar and some enormous *Abies pectinata*, the Common Silver Firs, almost impossible to grow nowadays because it is attacked by weevils; a monkey puzzle completed the picture.

Ellen Dunlop loved to watch the rabbits playing on the lawn, and none of these was allowed to be killed. When we arrived on the scene an enormous number of trees required to be felled in order to allow the sunlight to peep through the windows. The glorious grassy, heathery hills above the house were invisible until a barrier of chestnut trees was cut, and as for the walled garden, a great belt of trees, including enormous Cypresses, over-shadowed more than half its extent, making it well-nigh impossible to grow many of the plants we hoped would flourish. In the end, the trees which were necessary to be felled, paid for painting and papering the house!

So we moved in May while cuckoos called over and over again from their perches up on the hill, and soft white petals drifted in the breezes from the old cherry tree that leaned across the burn beside the stable yard. It was so exciting to have a home of our own again where the boys could dam the little burns that flowed everywhere, and where they could make endless runs for bantams, ducks, turkeys and all the rest. Bryce could rear his pheasants and replant the desecrated woodlands, which had been cut during the war years. Shelter belts were much needed, for the winds were strong and fierce, and winter long and very cold. Huntfield was built on the north side of the hill a thousand feet above sea level; from the top of our hills one could see the silver thread of the Clyde weaving its devious course between the solitary height of Tinto and the grassy steeps of Quothquan Law, which means the White Hill; and on the great river flows to Lanark, tumbling down the great waterfalls below Corehouse. On a clear day the Forth Bridge can also be seen from the top of these hills.

The garden had so many possibilities. A finely wrought iron gate in a gothic-shaped arch led into the walled area; this had been made by Miss Anderson of Barskimming in Ayrshire, a friend of Ellen Dunlop's, whose hobby it was to make such things of beauty assisted by her local blacksmith. A huge well-head was the centre-piece of a rose garden at the foot of the lawn on the north side of the house. The walled garden consisted of vegetables and fruit bushes and a herbaceous border in which there were a few seldom-seen old fashioned plants. Outside the wall, almost in the wood, was a border full of enormous clumps of the unusual *Veratrum nigrum*, a plant which I had never seen before, which seed themselves in the wonderful peaty soil at Huntfield. If the altitude was not so great we could grow almost anything, but we soon found that most shrubs needed protecting from the winds until they became well established.

The garden flourished, and the small greenhouse produced a wealth of seedlings; our ponies produced an abundance of manure which mulched the borders, but many plants usually taken for granted, such as hybrid tea roses, find it difficult to survive the rigorous climate for more than a few seasons; one learns to be selective in what one tries to grow.

Tom Moffat, a retired railway worker, bicycled up from Thankerton once or twice a week to help me, and after his death, Davy Anderson has come faithfully from Carnwath at weekends for many years. Otherwise we gardened ourselves. Daffodils and snowdrops are always magnificent and the garden has been opened to the public on many occasions in aid of the Queen's Nurses, the Thistle Foundation for disabled ex-servicemen, and for the Church. We worked very hard but it was worth every minute of effort. I grew the seeds and the plants, Bryce cut the lawns and kept the edges, and the boys helped; they mowed the grass beautifully. Eventually we bought a machine upon which they could sit, so that mowing the lawns and the many paths around our woodland gardens ceased to be such a toil.

Rabbits and roe deer were perpetual enemies. The former were, and still are, a never ending menace despite the ravages of myxamatosis which must have been a terrible scourge to the rabbit population. Nowadays rabbits frequently sleep above ground and the fleas which live in the burrows and carry the disease are of little avail. One has to adapt one's gardening outside the protected areas to growing shrubs and plants which are of no interest to such creatures. There are a number of herbaceous plants and shrubs which we discovered are safe to plant: among these are forget-me-nots, peonies, bearded iris, and their tough, thin-leaved Japanese varieties; heathers, lambs' lug, catmint, and the blue Himalayan poppies for which the Huntfield garden became well known; all sorts of primulas survive, although I have watched rabbits nipping off the coloured flowers of the candelabra varieties; but since primulas seed easily in the peaty soil, they are a "must". Strangely, *Viburnum fragrans* and maples appear safe to plant, but it is as well to protect them with rabbit netting when young. Shrub roses of the thorny kinds such as the lovely wine coloured Roseraie de l'Hay, which makes a spreading bush, or the pink Frau Dagmar Hastrap and the lovely Sarabande, are other good propositions;

also azaleas and rhododendrons. The beautiful hornbeam hedge we planted with such care and which became a wind-break of great beauty, fell a victim to the rabbits one recent very hard winter: this was a sad loss. Artichokes and potatoes take no harm, while raspberries produce wonderful crops if protected, though strangely, their wild counterparts grow like weeds among the rhododendrons and are untouched by the verminous rabbits. Since labour was very limited, beyond what we could accomplish ourselves, one learnt to adjust one's dreams of splendour and colour to reality, and most necessary of all, to the climate.

*   *   *

The years passed all too quickly, and when my father died in 1972, Dalemain and all its fair lands and well kept woodlands became our responsibility, ours to love and to cherish, and to continue to try and protect this great heritage, burdened by estate duties, for our children, and for the generations yet unborn; and to try, as the years slip past, to hand it on to the next generation in a better state, if possible, than it had been passed on to me.

Our life became one of many journeys, for our two homes and our two gardens were almost one hundred miles apart, and though in the past years we had farmed some of the land in Cumbria, as the years went by and my Father became older and less able to manage, we came to bear an increasingly larger share of the responsibilities. Fortunately our family were no longer children since it was necessary for us to travel the wearisome journey every week, spending three days in one home and four in the other; there was so much to be done in both, and one needed to adjust oneself to each environment quickly at the end of every journey. But somehow we managed. In those past carefree years, I always gardened at Dalemain whenever we stayed there, pruning shrubs and rambling roses, and caring for plants which were permanent and would otherwise have been neglected; but now it was different, and the garden almost became my *raison d'être*, while Bryce, later assisted by Robert who took over the farming enterprises, struggled to keep the estate solvent.

Robert was a true countryman, and when he left Huntfield and moved to Dalemain, lorry loads of antiquated farm machinery, pony traps, and farm wagons moved too, in order to reform his agricultural museum in the great barn across the courtyard, together with quite a little flock of sheep which he had gathered together.

The old house and its lovely acres has in a sense always "owned" the family rather than the other way round, since the days when Sir Edward Hasell bought the manor house and its lands in 1679. Each succeeding generation has tried in some way to improve the estate, or when times were bad, as so often happened, they just hung on grimly and hoped, like Mr. Micawber, that something better would turn up.

The hanging woodlands on the limestone escarpments that shelter the green acres in the parklands; the steep fell sides and rolling grassy summits where the red deer and Swaledale or Herdwick sheep feed above the silver ribbon-like stretches of Ullswater, are still part of the estate; but above all, there is the garden which is my heart's delight. This has evolved and grown with the house and its long history.

Dalemain was first recorded as a pele tower in the reign of Henry II. It was built on a bank suitable for defence at a point where the Dacre Beck joins the River Eamont two miles from Ullswater. In those days, vegetables and herbs would be grown of necessity, probably where they are still grown, in a small walled garden with the high wall of the Deer Park behind its eastern border.

A hall was added to the tower and later rooms were built above the hall and on to each end of the mediaeval building until it became an 'E' shaped house, fashionable in those days in order to honour the Faery Queen. An early eighteenth century house completed the square. The stone used for this is pale pink ashlar quarried nearby, which has weathered to a beautiful colour.

The garden had also grown with the years. Sir Edward Hasell improved the terrace walk and the borders he found there in 1679, and his diary tells of how he built the walls around his orchard and of all the men who worked for him, many of whose descendants with the same names are still living in the neighbouring villages.

Some of the walls in the garden were already there. These are made of very early brick which would have been made upon the site with wood fires; against them Sir Edward planted apricot trees which he brought back from London with him in 1687. Although he felt quite ill after the rough journey, he rose from his bed to see that they were properly planted in his orchard.

These walls would be heated to keep the late frosts off the blossom. A Knott garden made of low clipped boxwood was planted in varying formal shapes, possibly by the Layton family who had lived at Dalemain for many generations until it was purchased by Sir Edward. The high walls of his orchard were extended up the gradual slope beyond the Knott Garden somewhere about the end of the seventeenth century and were faced with pale pink ashlar, the old rough stone being visible from behind. A summer-house was built at the top of the garden in an archway in the wall, with oak seats carved in the style of William and Mary, upon which were painted fruits and flowers, still to be seen on some of them.

In the opposite corner is a much earlier summer-house, or gazebo, built in the early 16th century. Its pointed roof is supported with the original oak trusses centralising on a king post; a heavy lock on the studded door and corresponding ironwork is also of this date. The mullioned windows with latticed ironwork look out across the park with the beck flowing along merrily below the steep bank upon which this part of the walled garden has been created. This summer-house could be seen in the distance from the house, and its occupants could view everything from their vantage point. They would see the Coach Road traversing the park, and the horses pulling their heavy loads up the steep hill, sheltered by oak trees in Langfield Wood. At this point the road disappears from view, and the travellers would be lost from sight as the coaches rumbled down the gentle slope on the other side of the hill, to the lake. Summer-houses of this date were always built at vantage points for it was an isolated life in the countryside of the North of England, and travellers were made very welcome.

In the wall between the two summer-houses, is a door leading into the most beautiful of woods, known as "Lobb's Wood", so called by my mother who admired the works of J. M. Barrie and his much loved play "Dear Brutus". The strange little man, Lobb, gave the characters in the play their second chance in life; and so, too, when we open the door into this fairy-like wood where ferns and violets snuggle up against the tree trunks, and when we follow the mossy paths that wind above the beck, we feel a sense of peace and elation, and a certainty that by passing through the doorway, we too will be given a second chance.

In the days of the second Edward, known as Blackcap, and his illustrious mother Dorothy who was left a widow for many years, times became much grander. The Low Garden, situated between the terrace walk and the beck, was laid out in a formal style, and the parkland was landscaped. Herr Zwingler, whose family had come from the Dutch-German border to drain the Fenland at the time of the Restoration of Charles II, became a landscape gardener, and arrived at Dalemain in order to carry out the improvements in the manner of Capability Brown. Lime trees were planted in the park on the slopes beyond the river giving the impression of sweeping curves, while boundary screens of oak, beech, and Scots pine crowned focal points.

The river Eamont, winding its way from Ullswater through the parkland, was dammed up to form a small lake, and a bridge was built at a strategic point below the weir, the pillars being built of the same pale pink stone of which the front of the house was made. Water, being the most interesting object in the landscape, always captivates and refreshes the eye. A woodland walk was planted along the far side of the river in Grandiscar, with horse-chestnuts, silver firs (*Abies pectinata*) and beeches, where a few ancient yew trees already grew. At its eastern end, above the miller's house and the eel ark, the path led to an enormous oak tree known as the King Oak, which had been planted at an earlier date. A circular seat round the trunk of this ancient tree made a pleasant place for the ladies to pause in their walks; they planted drifts of snowdrops nearby which still shine like stars in February above the dark passage of the ever-moving river. The King Oak ended its long years about 1930 when it either blew down in a gale or was felled by my Father; his chief interest was in forestry and he liked to cut trees at the right time rather than to leave them for their aesthetic value.

Those gracious days are long since gone, and when my Father died we were left with an estate crippled by capital transfer tax, and a dear old house which needed much repairing, particularly to the roof. Our only course was to open its doors to the many visitors who holiday in the Lake District, and with much determination and carefully planned organisation, we welcomed the first visitors at Easter time in April 1977. Bryce ably took charge of the rocking ship and gave everyone who worked on the estate a feeling that all would be well. His wartime naval career stood us all in good stead, and without his abilities and calmness in those troubled days the "ship" could easily have been lost.

At one time Bryce wondered if we would have to abandon the garden, but I was determined to keep it going. Joe Rayson who had worked on the home farm and estate for a quarter of a century was our sole help in the garden at that time, and he and I "carried on". Since then, he has retired but comes one day a week in return for Snuff Mill, an enchanting lattice-windowed cottage in the park where snuff was once produced. Brian Pedder, a cheerful character, now gardens in his stead four days a week.

Meanwhile the garden improved visibly. The high garden that stretches up the slope to the summer houses was gradually cleared of vegetables, fruit bushes and weeds, and replaced with lawns and borders and a low curved wall half way up the slope to break the monotony. This wall and its wide steps were built by Joe, an expert dry-stone dyker, asssisted by Robert, our son, who had lately come to live at Dalemain. The long early vegetable border that extends from the Victorian greenhouses and the Knott Garden to the summer house, was filled with old-fashioned shrub roses and groups of low growing plants and bulbs, none of which should need to be staked. The kitchen garden behind the potting sheds was cultivated once more; it had become a wilderness in the last years, but fruit bushes, sweet peas and vegetables held their own once more. A small wheelhorse tractor was ordered at the Highland Show, and our old Merry Tiller went up and down the road at intervals behind the car in order to help to till both gardens. There had been no mechanisation of the garden previously. Barrowloads of manure had been pushed laboriously up the hill or through the door from Lobb's Wood, whereas now a machine would take the backache out of these necessary tasks.

The visitors give us much pleasure and satisfaction. They admire the house and the bowls of flowers, while the priest's "hidey-hole" in the thickness of the mediaeval walls gives them quite a thrill. But the garden brings untold joy, and many visitors return several times in a year to see it in the changing moods of the seasons. Sometimes, when I am working with the plants, I am taken for the gardener, and many amusing anecdotes could be told: one man "hoped I was being well paid!" The garden becomes alive and lived in, and there is a point in working long hours day after day when it is giving so many people pleasure.

Back at Huntfield in the quiet of our Scottish garden, close to the sound of the grouse calling "go-back, go-back" on the hills above, and the chatter of the wild geese flying in their hundreds on winter days, one renews one's strength and refreshes one's spirit, so that we can tend to the needs of two much loved homes.

*   *   *

There is no end or beginning to the gardening year; the whole of creation is in a circle, and seedtime and harvest follow one another in all too rapid a sucession. The older one grows, the faster the year turns, except when it is

February gold: aconites in the Grove.

Snowdrops and aconites carpet the woodlands that surround the walled garden at Huntfield.

The Knott Garden filled with herbs, violas and all manner of sweet smelling flowers, shadowed by the varied roofs and chimneys of the rambling medieval house.

A colourful corner in high summer where the shrub rose "Prince Charles" and chimney-pot campanulas grow in abandon.

winter and cold becomes increasingly hard to bear, especially in the north of the country where winter must be prepared for, and the garden and one's most tender plants must be covered carefully. An early spring can be even more than treacherous, leaving behind it a trail of saddened blossom, blackened by a sudden late frost.

By this time of year there is a quiet about the gardens, different from any other time of the year. The honk of the heron sounds hollow as he rises from the pool below the summer-houses and wings his way slowly above the Dacre Beck where cold mists foretell a frosty night. Blackbirds skim past one at dusk into the safety of the yew trees in a secretive way so that they may find their roosting places unseen by the predatory owl who has already begun to call from the little wood behind the barn.

The garden slips away into the unseen; the outline of boxwood hedges stand regimented around the mirrored pool, and darkened branches of apple trees are pencilled against the light of the half moon, riding roughly through coloured clouds.

Tools are hung up in their nightly places on rows of long nails driven into a board that has hung for many a year on the whitened walls of the potting sheds.

Evening and the dusk come early; it is time for that delicious hot cup of tea, and to sit on the little stool in front of a big log fire, toasting one's back; time to dream, and time to think of all one can do in the coming year; how one can improve this border and that corner; how one can succeed with the seeds which failed to germinate for lack of warmth; and of the old days, long ago, when generations of gardeners held sway and stoked their boilers before bedtime on such a night as this. A shadow passed the green door that opens on to the cold frames. The ice cracked on the deep water tank beside the stone steps that lead into the greenhouses. One could hear it clearly in the stillness of the frosty evening. The shadow might have been old Will Stuart on his rounds to see that all was safe.

It was from Stuart that I learnt my gardening lore. He was a wonderful person; born on Penicuik House estate, he served his time in the gardens at Taymouth Castle, and then as a journeyman in the famous Princes Street Gardens in Edinburgh. He came to Dalemain as head gardener in 1891 when the gardens were very beautiful. Aunt Maude, my Irish great-aunt, wrote in her diary the following spring that "the new gardener grew wonderful camelias".

As a little girl I followed Stuart around frequently sitting on an upturned bucket to watch him sow seeds in his cosy potting shed. There were always fine mixtures on his bench full of leaf mould which were fun to run through one's fingers. An extra boy from Moor End farm was taken on in the autumn to gather leaf mould into a long four-wheeled barrow which he and the under-gardener, Bill Slee, could manipulate across the river bridge from Grandiscar; they wheeled load upon load of the best food of all for the garden.

I watched Stuart prune the roses on the terrace long ago. "What are you doing, Stuart?" I was reputed to have asked. "Pruning, Miss Sylvia". "When will the prunes be ripe?'' This remark, made by a very small girl was never forgotten and always seemed to cause much amusement; it was *also* well remembered that the nursery had milk pudding and prunes regularly for Monday's lunch because it was baking day and innumerable loaves of crusty bread were rising in the bread oven. It was understandable how prunes and pruning became entangled with one another.

Stuart was never too hurried to talk to a little girl. "Five sweet pea seeds in a five inch pot" he would say. I watched what he did and never forgot. The enormous fairy pockets, as we called the calceolarias, that grew unfailingly in clean clay pots on the gravelled slabs in the hothouse; begonias of all sorts; but most beautiful of all, the small pink winter-flowering begonia, Gloire de Lorraine; – sweet scented lilies in pots were grown specially for the house; huge heads of *Lilium auratum*, the Gold Rayed Lily of Japan, that scented the drawing room. Mother had a large oak tub with a tin lining specially made in which they could stand, so that their pots would not mark the drawing room carpet.

At Christmas time Stuart and his under-gardener decorated the house; the kitchen, the front hall, and right up the staircase; every portrait within reach had a spray of holly perched on top of its gilded frame. The Old Hall, in the mediaeval part of the house, was garlanded with holly and ivy, for there, everyone came and went and toasted themselves by the big fire. Wreaths were made for "the graves" up in Dacre Churchyard, or big holly crosses; none of the dear departed were ever forgotten at Christmas or at Easter time.

Stuart died when I was twenty and it was a sad day when the old man was laid to rest with the others. He was taken up to the quiet churchyard on the dray, pulled by Daisy the black Clydesdale mare who was all groomed and polished for the occasion. She pulled the dray along the Holmes, the estate road that ran through the meadow lands beside the beck, and up to the gates of the ancient square-towered north-country church. Old Will's friends on the estate bore the coffin, and we sadly laid him to rest; the plaintive calls of the peewits from the ploughed lands close by dulled the pangs of sadness.

The seasons wait not for the whims and fancies of mankind. The restless urgencies of the awakening earth move on all too fast into the full glory of blossom time. We have scarcely had time to be fully aware of the wondrous beauty of the spring when the golden grain is standing tall and deep as if the carpet of ploughed furrows had never been there. Soon the wild winds blow again and the miracle of frost and snow fertilizes the ground, splitting the particles of earth so that it can be worked once more into a fine tilth where the roots of tiny seeds can find a foothold in yet another spring.

To be at one with all things appertaining to the countryside, one must always be ready to learn, and perhaps above all, to be quiet, so that one can think, and dream, and perhaps most important of all, one learns to understand.

* * *

A FEW INTERESTING ITEMS
RECORDED FROM EIGHTEENTH CENTURY VOUCHERS

		£	s.	d.
1772	Bot of Thos. Todhunter			
	Bill and Receipt for Hardware for 1 year	6	19	5¾
	incl. 1 pr garden shears		2	8
	1 qt. Linseed oil		1	–
	Round twine			5
	Scythe stone			3
	1 garden spade		3	4
Aug. 1	1 new suit for the gardener		2	6
Oct.	Christopher Thompson, Seedsman, for garden seeds	1	7	11½
1773				
Feb. 16	11 Matts for the garden		3	–
Jul. 14	14 Cartful of peat at 12d.		14	–
	To the Common gardener at Penrith for flower seeds		6	–
Sep.	Chris Thompson for a parcel of garden seeds	1	5	3
	Arthur Walker for different sorts of Flower Seeds		6	–
1774				
Jan.	Ann Dent for various books and magazines, and			
	The Wonders of Nature and Art. 6 vols. at 3/6d.	1	1	–
1782	Voucher 124			
	Messrs. Isaac Todd, Gardener at Dalemain			
	from Christopher Thompson (Nurserymen)			
	20 drop apples	1	–	–
	20 Fulberts		3	4
	1 drop D'Orr Plum		1	–
	1 Morrono Plum			
	20 Fine large new kinds of Gooseberrys		10	–
	Apples	1	16	11½

Apples
    4 Ribstone Pippins
    2 Golden Rennets
    2 Margells
    2 Nonsuch
    2 Golden Pippins
    2 Codlings
    2 Aikham Russett
    2 Sum^n Pearmain
    2 Borpuells

Gooseberries
    2 Golaak
    2 Nonsuch
    2 White Bellmount
    3 Little John
    2 White Lion
    2 Alexander
    2 Robin Hood
    2 Sydals Tupp

2 Golden Drop
1 Beamoemt

Ma 7½d½ Cge to Darlington

Farm Seeds Mixture Voucher No. 135
M & J Callender, Nurserymen and Seedsmen at the
Orange Tree, Middle Street, Newcastle.
(The voucher is stamped with an orange tree)

7 Stone fine cow grass at 8s.	£2	16	–
7 Stone White Dutch Clover at 7s.	2	9	–
7 Stone Trefoil at 3s.	1	1	–
3 New Canonss Baggs		3	6
	6	9	6

Thomas Nicholson
For making 150 roods of Open Drain 7′6″ wide at
the top, 4 ft. wide at Bottom, and 4 ft. deep from
Orchard down Carr towards Starling Bridge, and
from said Drain up the Beck to Mr. Wallace
ground near the Church

Thos. Robinson
For making Ha Ha Wall from Court towards Bridge
3ft. high at 9°   9   6

Nov. 1 Henry Hodson   2s.6d. for making a ditch from Ha Ha
End to Dacre Beck 3 ft. wide, 3 ft. 6 deep about
12 yards long   2   6

1769
Oct.   Dr. Harrison's Bill for drugs etc. incl. Rhubarb Infusion   9 12 11

1772   The Mowers, Will Hudson, Thos. Carlile, John
Stockdale for mowing all the land for grounds   15 10   –

1797
Jan. 28   Geo Armstrong & Thos. Robinson
The garding woall, 12 rood   1   7   0

1796
Apr. 23   Ye garding woalls coping
Dressing Copes
Laying the same
Pointing the said woalls at 2s. 0d. per day
Apr. 23   1 day   2   0
       25   4 ½ days   9   0
May 7   6 days   12   0
       14   6 days   12   0
       21   3 days   6   0
                                                                        2   1   0

May 5   Wm. Watson at 2s. 4d. per day
Ye garding woalls pointing and copeing the
same, 6 days   14   0

There are many bundles of vouchers tied up with string or pink linen tape of earlier years which are yet to be read. Some of the spelling is a little difficult to understand, and this has been copied letter for letter, but the items listed are of great interest in connection with the history of the garden.

The apples and gooseberries would be collected from Darlington by another carrier and brought to Dalemain. The Codlings are almost certainly the Keswick Codlings still bearing excellent fruit in the garden.

During the eighteenth century, the family owned a house called Woodford in Essex and possibly the fruit trees came from that area. Edward Hasell was living at Woodford at this time, while his older brother, Williams, known as "The Planter", was happily planting woodlands at Dalemain. His portrait, painted by the now famous local artist, Arthur Devis, hangs in the Chinese drawing room. He is depicted standing beside his beloved trees with his King Charles spaniel at his feet, and the Cumbrian fells in the background.

This Edward, grandson of Sir Edward Hasell who bought the earlier house from Madame Layton, was known as The Dutchman, since he spent much of his time in the Low Countries where he sold some of the family plate, in order to pay off part of the mortgages accrued by his father in the building and furbishing of the new part of Dalemain.

A YEAR BETWEEN TWO GARDENS

A Gardening Diary

Dalemain. The end of the calendar year draws nigh but there is still much that can be done before the year turns. We were always taught to clear up and to finish all the tasks one could before the bells rang the old year out. It was still open weather and a good time to cover the borders with manure. The long herbaceous border on the terrace had been forked through in November, and a layer of manure will protect the plants from bitter winds; much of it will have worked its way into the ground before spring.

Tulips are already poking their noses up in sheltered patches. The pheasants cause untold damage, strutting along the terrace and digging down into the bulbs, leaving a miserable shoot and the shell of a bulb in their wake. Prickly holly leaves and sprigs of such things as berberis are said to deter mice and pheasants from attacking bulbs. A layer of these held down by a few stones might help, but if one did all the things one ought to do one would never finish.

Wednesday 19th Put a few cloches on the various clumps of Christmas roses already showing pinky-white flowers; their stems gradually unbend themselves as they are freed from the soil. A little protection keeps the wet and the snow from ruining their petals, but plenty of fresh air must be allowed to circulate. Some of the present plants must be moved to more sheltered corners later on; the best plants seem to grow behind a low holly hedge where the summer sun is unable to dry them out. A generous blanket of leafmould in November encourages them to root freely.

Friday 21st Planted some new shrubs at the top of the garden in a somewhat draughty corner. When they grow, they will help to break the wind that romps round a very tall Norway maple and some equally tall oak trees growing on the Wild Garden bank close to the Tudor summerhouse. A good specimen of *Cotoneaster salcifolia* was planted and firmly staked. Behind this and already growing strongly, are several tough thorny *Rubus cockburnianus*, the ornamental bramble, whose young canes look as if they have been white-washed, and a hedge of mixed *Cotoneaster simonsii* and boxwood grown from seedlings and cuttings. Although still young the hedge is beginning to give a little much needed shelter to this corner.

December
Saturday 22nd   A large *Stransvesia* planted a little lower down the border last year is growing well. This was my sister's Christmas present a year ago; we always give each other shrubs on such occasions. The nursery garden at Appleby had many small *Stransvesia* plants on that occasion, but we took the chance with this four foot container-grown specimen. With lots of leaf-mould used in the planting and stamping the earth firmly round its roots, it looked secure. Some of its leaves had already turned red and gold, brightening the darker side of this part of the garden, where ancient yews, planted at a lower level in the Wild Garden long, long ago, shade the border. A new Golden Queen holly found a sheltered sunny home at the foot of the bank below the yews. Hollies are really woodland trees, needing the protection of their neighbours, and since gardens should be places of beauty at all seasons, what can be more lovely than variegated hollies. This particular plant was Etta Murray's Christmas present; each year she gave us a garden token, and though our old friend is failing fast, the golden holly will stand as her memorial for generations to come.

Monday 24th   *Huntfield.*   Back at Huntfield for the Christmas festival and to the joy of having little David Andrew, our first grandchild, living so close to us in "the other half" of the house. Christmas seems to be even more wonderful and ethereal when there is a new baby in the house, and grandparents are often useful people to have at hand!

Planted a low growing shrub, the Partridge Berry, near the little pool; peaty conditions are essential, and though the climate is much, much harder than it is at Dalemain, I hope this Christmas present to the garden will survive. In the past so many shrubs have been planted outside the walled garden, but unless strongly netted the thousands of rabbits who live on the surrounding hills and fields play havoc with most of them.

Tuesday 25th   There really were Christmas roses in the garden at Huntfield; not very big or long-stemmed, but their flowers, so precious at this time of year, were pushing their way to the light, the grey vein-like lines in their fleshy white petals contrasting the light and shade from the weak morning sunshine. An occasional and somewhat small polyanthus was also in bloom and some frosted sprays of jasmine, hanging limply against the garden wall.

Wednesday 26th   Must remember to prune the jasmine properly after it flowers, but up here, since it blooms intermittently over a long period, it never seems to be the right time to give it a good clipping.

The real glory of the garden is the *Viburnum fragrans*, the Bodnant variety. It grows on the outside wall of the garden to gain as much shelter as possible, where a huge old hawthorn gives some protection from the frost. The sumptuous pink flower heads growing on the second-year wood are so prolific this winter and cause quite a splash of colour even from a distance, while the scent is quite delicious.

December When the better weather returns, more suitable for planting, I must lift some of the suckering growths of this Viburnum and transplant them nearer to the house in both gardens where we can all revel in this winter fantasy — these dreamlike flowers of mid-winter. The old variety is more troubled with the frost and wintry conditions and the blossoms frequently look quite brown.

Friday 28th Winter arrived with a vengeance and Huntfield was soon covered in its usual blanket of snow. Over the years one learns to live with the elements and not fight against the impossible. There is so much for which to be thankful. If it were not for the protection of snow, the cruel winds and hard frosts would kill many of the smaller plants. More tender shrubs must be protected for several winters after planting, with home-made wigwams of spruce branches firmly tied to a tripod of stakes with binder twine, lately discarded from the bales of hay fed to the ponies. Outside the kitchen window the now huge red maple, *Acer palmatum atropurpureum*, fills me with immense pride. For about six winters after planting, it was covered with a "wigwam" by which time it was well established and has never looked back.

Magnolias need the same treatment. As the shrubs grew taller and wider, the wigwams became much too small and four rounded spruce posts with cross-bars nailed firmly became the order of the day. With a tall step-ladder and armfuls of fir branches, I perched perilously while covering the topmost branches, allowing the fir to hang well over the edge, then tied everything firmly down. It is important to leave the winter covering *in situ* till the last frosts of the season are past; thus *Magnolia wilsonii* produces a wealth of blossom which always surprises gardening friends in the area.

Our cup was filled with happiness for a second time when Robert, our dear, middle son, announced his engagement to Jane Halsey just before Christmas. Robert has always been a country boy and now he is in charge of farming operations at Dalemain, as well as keeping a watchful eye upon everything that takes place on the estate. Now he and Jane will have the fun of making a home together and a garden full of flowers at Dalemain.

Monday 31st *Dalemain.* We were back at Dalemain for the next few days. The air was crystal clear with hard frost and much snow. The sun shone out of a clear blue sky by day. The waters of the Eamont sparkled in the distance and apple trees were silhouetted against the blue sky, their branches covered in frozen snow. What a wonderful day to take a ciné film. It was perfect filming, with the arches of the yew trees making picture frames, while the snow-clad fells above Ullswater stood out in the distance beyond the park.

The pink flowers of the Viburnum were extremely photogenic as were the hart's tongue ferns, nestling against the orchard wall, while in sheltered places, an early aconite peered out from its white blanket, its frilly green collar holding high the golden flower bowl. Sometimes these films are very useful when I am asked to talk to some organisation about our gardens, or about the history of Dalemain. Down beside the river, the reeds and long grasses were

December covered with glinting icicles and the dark surging waters hurried under the humpy bridge that carried the coaches long ago safely across the Dacre Beck.

Back in the house, it was time to think about ordering flower seeds. Each year I intend to grow fewer half-hardy annuals which need pricking out and much attention; but one has so many favourites that it is hard not to continue sowing them. Nemesia and the sweet scented heliotrope are some of these. The latter was grown as standard plants by Stuart in the days gone by, underbedded with clear yellow calceolarias, while huge beds of perfectly grown nemesia in the gardens at St. Annes-on-Sea were a never-to-be-forgotten sight. As children, we sailed our boats in the ponds in these gardens near the sea front, where evening primroses grew wild on the sand dunes; but the formal beds of nemesia and their wondrous rainbow coloured flowers will always remain in my memory. Tagetes is another useful annual making a showy edging to a dull corner, and if there is time to grow another half-hardy annual, kingfisher daisies give enormous pleasure, but need a sunny situation to give of their best.

January
Thursday 3rd *Huntfield.* The air smelt of change, and surely enough, by evening the thaw had set in. Birds were moving about more freely in the bushes, and the ponies had found fresh grass at the very top of the field above the garden which adjoins the heather covered hill. Fell ponies will always search for grass when it is at all possible, leaving good hay untouched; nature calls them back to the open hills, but come a hard night they are back down to the refuge of their hay rack.

Friday 4th Covered the old clump of *Anemone hepatica* with a cloche. Nothing very much of them is showing at present but the gnarled knots of wakening shoots. Two lavender-blue flower buds were visible when I scratched away the short rotted manure that lay near in the border; their turned-over flower heads gave me a thrill, in the same way that the rush of spring and the awakening earth, surging through one's whole being, fills one's soul with excitement.

Saturday 5th When it was dark I went to turn on the heaters in the greenhouse. There had been a shoot, and it was quite likely that the rabbits would enter the garden through gates left unshut. As I walked round with a torch, it was quite exciting to see snowdrops and daffodils peeping through the dark earth. *Primula denticulatas* were stirring their grey-green rosettes beginning to take shape, and their small pointed leaves looking no more than an elfin's pointed cap.

Monday 7th The nights are suddenly drawing out; how amazing when the year has scarcely turned, but how exciting. On Saturday at the shoot, several people remarked on the lighter evenings, so I knew that my flights of fancy were not just wishfulness and that springtime was really on the way.

January
Tuesday 8th

Dalemain. The most beautiful Christmas roses were growing in the garden at Dalemain Mill. Jack and Edna Holliday had a vase of them on their table when we dined with them, arranged with *asparagus sprengerii.* Edna had so many of these welcome *Helleborus* that she brought us a bunch the next day.

Wednesday 9th

Looked again for our own Christmas roses which were still just showing. The *Helleborus foetidus* have grown into good plants further up the garden, again on the shaded side, and these were only planted a year ago. Their deeply cut leaves, like cart wheels, stand out elegantly on a dusk January evening.

Brian had already spread manure on quite an area of the borders; a good country smell and a protection against the cold winds of winter.

Thursday 10th

It was the Twelfth Night and the Christmas tree from the Old Hall was sadly cast outside, but rather than waste such a noble tree which had gladdened our hearts for three weeks past, it was cut up and used to protect shrubs in the Low Garden; firstly the lovely Japanese maple *Dissectum atropurpureum* which is beginning to grow at last and replenish its winter-worn branches – this is the third one to be planted at Dalemain, this specimen being a container shrub planted in July which I found in Murrell's nursery when I was down that way to judge ponies at the Royal Show – the other two having died in previous years. Another shrub needing protection was *Eucryphia Nymansay*; its two or three predecessors planted in the walled garden at Huntfield with the greatest of care, had likewise shrivelled and passed away. It is just too cold and high for them to survive. They are such beautiful trees, with their creamy white flowers that look like ballet dancers among glossy evergreen leaves in September and October; a time of year when few shrubs are in flower.

Friday 13th

Huntfield. Gaggles of wild geese, mainly pink feet with some barnacles and a rare snowgoose among their numbers, fly nightly across Huntfield from the peat hags on the top of Biggar Common where they spend their days. They drop down so cannily on the potato fields and upon some acres of barley which were never harvested on Whitecastle land; it had been a particularly wet autumn and a very difficult harvest time. The haunting cry of the wild geese, so usual to us up here, is something we still listen to as if we'd never heard it before; it is so hauntingly wonderful and so mysterious. They fly in a V-shape with a strong-winged leader well out in front. Small parties join the main flock, flying at a lower level until they too are drawn up into the main stream. All things in nature are so disciplined and orderly.

Damp snow blew quite strongly from the East and the countryside was white for a little while, but as evening drew on, the air was still and a clear and enormous star hung like a solitary lantern to guide us home along the twisting, walled road from Edinburgh. It might have been the star that guided the Wise Men to Bethlehem, looking so important and alone in the sky.

January
Tuesday 15th It was dark when I closed up the greenhouse and with my torch searched among the *Lenten hellebore* clumps for possible flowers. There they were, claret coloured stumpy flowers well through the soil on one large old plant and nothing showing among the others which are probably of a slightly different variety. Another winter treasure. No aconites to be seen as yet, and though they have been stirring for a long time past, they are somewhat late in flowering this year.

Wednesday 16th Picked some heathers to fill a posy vase for the table. Springwood White and Springwood Pink have given us tremendous pleasure for many years now: the former always appears to have green flowers when they are in bud; they are such useful winter flowers. Some of the original plant has been pulled apart and planted in other places at Huntfield, and some has established itself in the Low Garden at Dalemain, despite some lime problems in the soil. I must collect more heathers this year since the rabbits will not bother them and little bulbs can be grown amongst the rough growth, from which they gain protection. Some of these Ericas will tolerate small quantities of lime, and their many varieties can be obtained to flower at all times in the year.

Thursday 17th *Dalemain.* Over the Devil's Beef Tub and down to Moffat and on to Dalemain. Sharp frost in the morning, but considerably milder as the afternoon wore on. A parcel of strawberry plants had arrived from Ken Muir who advertises unusual varieties to prolong the fruiting season. I meant to heel them in but since the ground was quite soft I was able to plant them; ten Getto, eleven Grandis, and ten Pantuguella. Brian had cleaned out the soil compost in which the tomatoes had grown last year; this was rich, friable, and peaty, so a double handful was put round each new young strawberry plant to make them safer from the frost.

Friday 18th We had a good morning pruning apple trees and others which were in need of some large branches being cut out. Reg, who works on the estate in many capacities, was free to help with the power saw while Brian and I considered which branches should be cut, and propped the ladder safely for Reg to climb with the heavy saw. We cut innumerable cross branches and an enormous branch off an old cherry tree in the Low Garden which was ruining an ancient Bramley seedling on the other side of the path. A very tall and spindly elm on the bank was felled just right, avoiding the lately planted holly and azaleas, and an equally dangerous sycamore leaning over the Wendy House was brought down. While the going was good, Brian persuaded Reg to help him to get a load of dung from the farm so that he can start to dig next week.

A sharp frost fell as the evening darkened. The cuts made where branches were sawn off are to be painted next week with Stockholm tar or cuprinol to prevent water and disease from penetrating the cut surfaces. It is recommended nowadays that only the edges of the cut be painted instead of the entire surface.

Saturday 19th

JANUARY GOLD

I wandered in the wintry wood
Where tall and straight the chestnut stood,
Its curving branches bending low
To shelter all the ground below;
And there, with faces gold and bright,
My darling winter aconite.

Under the protection of the chestnut trees near the back door the aconites were showing their green frilly heads already. The peach trees in the greenhouses were showing tips of pink flower buds; a little more pruning was accomplished before nightfall. Living between two places makes it impossible to keep up to date with everything that should be done, besides being extremely exhausting.

Monday 21st   *Huntfield.*   Snow lay quite thickly in the early morning and the road back over Beattock was difficult. Collected about forty fish boxes from Jean Paul's shop for seedlings to be "pricked out" into later on; these boxes, smelling strongly of fish, must lie out to weather before use, otherwise they burn and kill the seedlings. It is such a help to get some new boxes each year. In Penrith it seems difficult to obtain them.

The birds were busy round their table. A cheese we were given at Christmas, and which we did not like, was pushed into a nut net, and this is proving very popular. Must make a bird pudding to hang up which will be composed of bread, dried fruit, and fats, and any suitable scraps. I'm sure that hand-feeding the birds in winter as so many people do, must save many tiny lives.

Tuesday 22nd   *Dalemain.*   As I motored along the edge of Ullswater on my way to Mrs. Clark's sewing class in Pooley Bridge, there were all manner of ducks bobbing up and down in the shallows of the lake. They sit on this part of water constantly, tufted, golden-eyed, coots, water hens and many more, their diving antics so fascinating to watch. There they sleep as well, since it is safer and warmer out on the water than it is for them to roost on the land.

Mrs. Clark is a wonderful person, who can teach us to upholster chairs, restore cane and rush-seated chairs, dress-make, create embroideries or anything we choose to do. There is so much furniture to repair and restore in Dalemain that these weekly classes are invaluable besides being a happy gathering of friends. The journey along the park and past the ancient hedgerows which grow beside the road leading down to the lake, has always something wonderful to look upon, whether it be clusters of early primroses, celandines and coltsfoot growing in sheltered crannies, or the ever-changing lights and shadows on the fell sides.

Finished pruning the peach and nectarine trees in the greenhouse. After fruiting when the leaves are beginning to drop, the new and unwanted young wood of the current season's growth is "summer pruned" – cut back half way to a bud – but any good young growth which might replace an older branch is retained and tied in place to grow where it is required, or used to fill in a gap on the wall. During the winter old fruiting wood is cut out, for the fruit is only borne on one-year-old wood. It is important that the branches have space to grow and are not overcrowded.

This is a somewhat laborious occupation, especially when pruning the fan-trained trees growing up the span of the greenhouse roof, but one which must be done. The back wall of the greenhouse now must be white-washed to clean it, and to show off the peach blossom which will break bud in a very short time.

Cut down all the old growths of the passion flower growing much too strongly, leaving only two or three young shoots which will quickly cover their allotted span of the wall in summertime. The top growth of the plumbago needed cutting back too, leaving some of the side growths to be taken as cuttings at the end of February.

It was a springlike afternoon and the garden smelt beautifully of life beginning to wake up again. More manure arrived from Park House and Brian was breaking up the concrete foundation of Geordie Pattinson's vast war-time rabbit hutch which he built in the kitchen garden; so now we can really dig and clean that dirty corner and put it back into rotation.

Thursday 24th
Mr. Noblett, the Horticultural Advisor at Newton Rigg, the Cumberland Agricultural College, walked round the garden with me in order to glean information for a pamphlet on gardens open to the public in Cumbria. We looked at everything, and I told him what I knew of the history of the garden; of the rare trees, herbaceous plants and shrub roses, and about our special plants.

There were aconites in bloom on the edge of the drive and among the azaleas at the end of the terrace. It was the most gorgeous day; a blackbird sang its first spring song from the holly tree at the corner of the house – quite wonderful. By afternoon there were more aconites in flower. They always fill me with wonder and excitement.

Friday 25th
Reg helped me while I gave the ponies worm doses in their field up the beckside. On the way back from the Langfields we filled sacks with beautiful leafmould from Nutchy Hill. This can be put on to the peach borders on top of the manure, and should do untold good. The leafmould was a mixture of beech and larch, crumbly with age, and easy to shovel up; we scarcely left a mark where we dug, there was so much woodland wealth on the forest floor.

January
Saturday 26th

Huntfield.   Freezing fog hung about all day, though the sun struggled to come through. Even the ponies' manes were white with strings of fog in the evening as they waited to get into their loose boxes for the night. The trees shone and sparkled in the veiled sunlight; wild geese called magically as they flew their accustomed route above the house, but hidden from view today, back to settle on the field of ungathered barley on Whitecastle farm and to gorge themselves before dark, leaving their haunts among the black peat hags for another day.

An azalea given to me as a Christmas present has flowered magnificently, but now as the last flowers fade it is time to keep it in the greenhouse where the moist atmosphere will encourage new growth. Daily spraying should help to prevent the leaves dropping.

Pine needles off the forest floor are sometimes used in the mixture when repotting. I always mean to try these since our pine trees grow on acid soil and should be highly beneficial to azaleas. When the Christmas cyclamen finish flowering, they too, go to some odd corner of the greenhouse to continue growing. During the summer they stand outside on their sides to rest until mid-August when new growth is appearing; they are then turned upright and soon after, brought indoors before the first frosts arrive; feeding every ten days commences at this stage.

Monday 28th

The seed cups of the azaleas in the Wild Garden at Huntfield still held innumerable tiny black winged seeds, so I decided to collect some and sow them in a wooden box hoping for a small forest of seedlings to germinate. The seed cups were brought indoors and crushed to release the seeds and later sown on to the surface of a compost of riddled forest litter to which a little coarse sand was added. The blue tits and other small birds had also filled themselves with seed but there was plenty left, and it gives so much satisfaction to try something different, and possibly have dozens of small hybrid azaleas to plant out in a few years time.

Tuesday 29th

Dalemain.   Back to Dalemain and a quick look round with Brian. He had put some whitewash behind the peaches, and although it looked very patchy, it will help to clean and disinfect the walls. A lot of ground has been manured, and we are really very well on, but even so, spring always comes with a rush. Aconites were blooming here and there. I must look down on the Low Garden bank where I transplanted some last spring and see if they have established themselves and are beginning to show their golden faces.

Wednesday 30th

A mild beautiful day. Brian and I went to Nutchy Hill with the little tractor and collected up bags of leafmould from under the young beech trees and larches. Beautiful stuff; one could cover the garden with it and do endless good. This collection was for the tomato beds, azaleas, seeds and new roses. The woods were so peaceful, and life was beginning to hum again.

Planted the new shrub roses from David Austin: Glastonbury and Mrs.

January   John Laing, in the "Children's Garden" – Commandant de Beaurepaire, The Squire, The Friar, and Shropshire Lass, nearby where not long since the rhubarb used to grow. It was rather sad to find that Lavender Lassie split off at the graft as I lifted her out of the bed into which the roses had been heeled. I wonder if it will grow again, but I planted her to give her a chance. The Children's Gardens are small flagged-edged plots on either side of the door into Lobb's Wood, with a little path running down the centre of each. Here, as a child I tried to grow all manner of little things long ago, in the same way that generations of children had done before my day. They were difficult little gardens with no water supply near, and there were constant journeys down the long sloping hill to the nearest tap with tiny watering cans; often there were broken knees from falling on the gravel as children constantly do because they run more often than walk, and are always in a hurry.

Thursday 31st   There was a strange almost eerie look about the evening sky last night. Brian thought something was brewing as that unwanted silence pervaded the countryside and banks of clouds began to gather over the East Fells. The morning was bitterly cold and the high village of Alston was already blocked by snow; snow was falling in Brampton and many other places and we became anxious for the return journey to Huntfield. As we crossed the Solway the most wonderful sunset filled the western sky and reflected the glory of its colours in the wide waters of the estuary and far beyond. The moon hung like a fiery ball in the night sky over the top of Quothquan Law as we turned up the twisted road above the Clyde; and when we reached home everything was blanketed in snow sparkling like myriads of diamonds in the moonlight.

February *Friday 1st*   Snow was falling much of the day and it was better to stay indoors. When last at the sewing class, learning to reseat and restore chairs, I asked if anyone knew any time-honoured sayings or rhymes for Candlemas-tide, most of the class being knowledgeable country people, wise in the lore of the land and observant of signs foretelling the weather. Mrs. Coulson, whose family have farmed Hole House Farm for a long time, remembered a verse as follows:

> *If Candlemas Day be clear and fair*
> *There'll be two winters in one year.*

From her farm house Mrs. Coulson has the most perfect view up the first "reach" of Ullswater as far as Hallin Hag with its ancient oak trees and up to the high tops of the Hellvelyn range peeping over Beda Fell. The ever-changing weather conditions are clearly visible from up the lake; below her farm the River Eamont flows, past Dunmallet's wooded rise and on to Dalemain; while on the other side of Hole House Farm, Mill Moor's gorse-covered acres are a sanctuary for nesting stonechats and wheatears. Across this small area of common land where adjoining farmers each have so many "rights" to graze stock, one right for a sheep, two for a cow, or three for a horse, the track lay from Pooley Bridge to Pooley Mill where in times gone by the miller ground corn to provide sustenance for both man and beast.

The other verse I remembered from long ago:

If Candlemas Day be bright and fair
Half the winter's to come and mair;
If Candlemas Day be dull and grey
The winter's worst is past and away.

Saturday 2nd
Candlemas Day It was a horrible day, with snow still falling steadily. My mind was still on country proverbs and I thought of yet another: "If the ice will bear a goose before Christmas, it won't bear a duck afterwards." This saying has frequently proved to be right, so we shall see if spring will come early this year, after unpleasant winters and late frost in the last years. A wintry fortnight in November is frequently a good sign for us in the North, but from time immemorial wise farmers have half their hay crop left untouched on Candlemas Day.

Monday 4th *Garrya elliptica* is making a wonderful show with long streamers of grey-green catkins cascading from the dark shining leaves. It is so important to grow something for every season of the year, and in a sheltered corner at the back of the delphiniums the garrya is an effective shrub. Three were planted at Huntfield in the days when shrubs cost very little, but the climate was too hard and only one survived, which has never produced catkins although it has a special corner, sheltered by redcurrants on the garden wall.

Gathered sprays of yew and holly from the Grove, the little wood close to the house on the edge of the lawn. These and other greeneries last well for flower decorations in vases around the house during winter time. Sprays of boxwood and mahonia, the latter bearing such beautiful shining copper-coloured leaves, and perhaps a little variegated holly, help to make the house look alive. These arrangements can be very attractive and yet so simple and economical. Sometimes sprays of hardwood trees such as elm, mixed with the darker evergreens, look almost more beautiful than if the same vase had been filled with coloured flowers.

Tuesday 5th Eight years ago the Grove was filled with ancient trees, including some ash trees which were liable to blow in winter's gales and fall on the barns and the joiner's shop which backed on to the little wood. For many years past Father was greatly worried every time the great ashes bent and swayed over the roof tops but Mother preferred the ancient walls hidden from sight, and the trees remained. In past days they certainly hid from view the well-worn path that led to the "privies" built into these walls behind the farmyard with convenient drainage. There were two "privies" and in one of them there were two full-sized wooden seats and one very small one for children, all most beautifully made. When Grandfather was a young man it was still considered proper for the gentlemen to walk down the Grove to use the privies even though his mother had installed the first water closets about 1830 in a specially built lavatory tower attached to the house. This tower was fondly known as "Grannie's wedding present"; it had two enormous lead tanks at the top which filled with rain water off the roof.

How delighted Father would have been to see the trees safely felled in frosty December weather when the ground was hard and the great boles hauled out of the wood without harming the aconites. An enormous sycamore close to the house was felled one evening and of necessity was left perilously, standing overnight until heavy enough tackle arrived to pull it over. If the wind had risen on that starry evening the house would have been badly damaged.

I was anxious that the grass would not take over to choke the carpet of aconites which completely carpets the wood at the turn of every year; they peep out on the edge of the drive where it turns the bend towards the courtyard and the farm buildings, and from every sheltered corner, to delight the eye. Each year, so far, after raking the rough branches and leaves off in the winter, the aconites have shone like gold to cheer the early weeks of the year.

We expect to see a few on New Year's Day, sheltered by the holly bushes in sunny places, but this year they are late, and only now their dear cheerful faces are appearing as the snow clears. Perhaps they will last longer this year and the tourists will be able to see them at Easter time. One lady told us that she would always remember Dalemain for this wondrous flower; other visitors to the district walk down the Church road from Dacre village especially to gaze upon this carpet of gold.

Wednesday 6th The Chinese Witch Hazel looks strong and looks beautiful flowering in the shelter of the Grove and the stable wall. I seem to remember that this variety is called Jelena, or Copper Beauty, having large spidery flowers which appear to be rich coppery red. Witch hazels will not grow in alkaline soils, and earlier plantings up the garden have suffered from liming the vegetable ground in past years, even though peat and leaf mould have been dug in generously. They are expensive shrubs to plant nowadays, so it was exciting to see Jelena looking so well.

Thursday 7th Finished pruning the gooseberries; gave them open centres and cleaner legs. They looked much better. Left all the prunings lying on the gravel on the snow till it clears when they can be raked away. Started to prune back the spurs on the old wall apples which are growing too far out. It will probably encourage young growth to emerge out of old wood. Pruned everything I could reach without a ladder. It is amazing how many little tasks one can accomplish even on wintry days.

Friday 8th It was a better day, so Brian and I finished pruning the wall apples with ladders, tying back some of the old framework on to the wires put along the

February   wall by Bill Goodwin twenty years ago. A green woodpecker yaffled off and on from the Langfield wood. It seems very early to hear them call, but old or dying trees are ideal hunting grounds for woodpeckers, and in a little while the great spotted woodpecker will be heard too, drumming with his beak in he nearby woods. Sadly the Dutch elm disease is killing some of the oldest of the elm trees, but up to date the younger ones have escaped the dreaded plague. In the meantime these dying trees are ideal haunts and shelter for woodpeckers.

As the snow melted rapidly, snowdrops and a few periwinkles emerged from under the shrubs, looking so fragile and beautiful.

Saturday 9th   What a wonderful freshness there seemed to be as the snow finally disappeared off the low ground. The grass looked greener, and as if it had grown under the protective covering, while aconites held their heads high as if to fill their petal bowls with every possible gleam of sunshine. One looked at everything in the gardens and the woodlands as if one had never seen them before. A few dark violet *Iris reticulata* appeared from under coverings of aubretia on the edge of the terrace border, and daffodil leaves arose like small green spearheads all over the grass in the Wild Garden. The birds seemed to take on a new lease of life; blue-tits, coal-tits and great-tits were performing gleeful acrobatics on the wire holding up halved coconuts below the bird table.

Monday 11th   Mahonia Charity is making a splendid show near the top of the garden, its handsome scented sprays of deep yellow reaching outwards and upwards as if to welcome the spring. The original old fashioned mahonia grows so easily and seeds itself under apple trees, and with its shiny bronze-green leaves and clusters of tiny yellow scented flowers is so useful for flower decoration in winter time. This is the time of year when it is really beneficial to prune some of it low, almost to the ground, to encourage young growth which makes good nesting places for warblers and other little birds. In the same way, the old yellow Rose of Sharon, growing under the dining room windows on the terrace benefits from being cut to the ground. Ususally half of its growth is cut one year and the rest the following spring so that it does not look too bare.

Tuesday 12th   Seeds all showing well, sown exactly a fortnight ago. Lifted the black polythene laid over the plastic propagators, and gazed in wonder at the first seeds of the year, antirrhinums, and penstemons; the latter take so long to mature and flower and need to be sown early in the year, or probably better still, the previous August.

Planted some of the new tea roses; the brilliant flame coloured Alexander (£1.20 a bush) which has somewhat replaced Superstar, near the top of the garden. The group of three will give a splash of colour similar to that of the tall shrub rose, Fred Loads, growing nearby. The second group of roses, planted near the corner of the low wall half way up the lawn was the dwarf red Tip Top at 95p a bush.

Sowed heliotrope and calceolarias, such small seed that no soil covering is necessary. They were watered "in" using a fine rose on the can. Plastic propagators are such a help, keeping the soil suitably damp and making further watering unnecessary until the seeds have germinated and rooted themselves into position.

Planted a group of three Silver Jubilee roses (£1.20 a bush) in front of the old rhubarb bed. Roses are nowadays so expensive that one must make the most of each variety by planting them in separate little groups among other types of plants, so that the beauty of each will not be lost among a whole variety of rose bushes.

Thursday 14th
St. Valentine's
Day The official first day of spring, at least among the birds in their woodland world; and so it was, a quiet day and full of sunshine, so different from last year on the same date. I went to the Langfield wood to place garden canes as markers where ten walnut trees are to be planted by Bill Lockerbie, our expert, semi-retired forester who comes to care for the woodlands three days a fortnight. The far end of the wood is a sad mess, devastated by rabbits, with some trees eaten and some non-existent. Here and there, beech and Scots pines that have survived are well up, and a group of very unusual oaks with barks similar to silver birches are thickening out. There were plenty of spaces to place the fine English Walnuts near the wood edge against the west park where they will be visible to future generations.

Walked on across the river into Grandiscar, to find a few more spaces for further special trees, a Wellingtonia, a Deodara Cedar, an American Beech, and a Balsam Poplar. Again there was plenty of room in the centre of this wood; it is intended to plant an arboretum along the woodland path above the river, but each special tree needs protecting since sheep sometimes find their way through an ancient post and rail fence, erected by Father about 1920 and still in working order. This was one of the first woodland fences he erected after he was demobilized in 1918. The posts and rails had been creosoted under pressure, and are still in reasonable condition sixty years later.

Friday 15th *Huntfield.* Went to Edinburgh on the most beautiful warm sunny day. Yellow crocuses were already blooming under the fine trees in Ainslie Place, and jasmine, blooming like stars of the morning, in all the little gardens. Too good a day for the city when one ought to have been gardening.

Saturday 16th So mild and sunny it was like an April day. Little wrens popping in and out of their winter quarters among the trellis at the end of the garden where there is plenty of shelter. Such beautiful, game little birds. In the terrible winter of 1967 many of the wrens and other small birds simply snuffed it; tree creepers were hit particularly badly, and since then, are seldom seen at Huntfield.

February
Sunday 17th   Davy had left some good soil in the open part of the potting shed which he had collected from mole hills, so it was quick work to make a mixture with leaf mould, sharp sand, an ounce of limestone, and an ounce of superphosphates per bushel of the mixture, for seed sowing. Sowed onions, (Bedfordshire Champion and Ailsa Craig), tomato (Ailsa Craig), lettuce, cauliflower, Greyhound cabbage, and pansies. Before doing this I had taken the window brush, hot water and Jeyes Fluid to spring-clean the glass and the woodwork in order that the greenhouses might be relatively bug-free. Jeyes fluid is most economical and beneficial to plant growth.

Monday 18th   Some of the apple trees were sprayed with tar-oil winter wash, but the knapsack sprayer was not working properly thus handicapping proceedings greatly. The sweet pea trenches were finished and filled with manure, six weeks later than usual, but only now the ground is beginning to dry up after months of wet weather. We always try to open the trenches by New Year to allow the frost to penetrate before filling them in. Bone Meal should also be put on at this time, remembering that it takes six months before it can be assimilated by the plants. Three weeks before planting sweet peas, a dressing of superphosphates is given. These instructions were given to me by me grandmother's gardener many years ago. I have never seen such sweet peas as the ones he grew in the walled garden above the spacious waters of the river Teith at Lanrick Castle, near Callender.

Tuesday 19th   *Dalemain.*   Back at Dalemain with fish boxes in the boot of the car for sweet pea seeds; and a bag of sharp sand and one of moss, so that the mixture could be made more quickly since there was no sharp sand readily available. Made a nice friable mixture. The mole hill soil and the leaf mould from Nutchy Hill was nice to work with. Filled a number of seed boxes and pans and left them for the morrow. A good covering of moss on the bottom of each box will help to keep the mixture damp, and using very hot tap water to water the boxes before sowing, heats the mixture and kills off some of the bugs. Soaked sweet pea seeds overnight in water. Some varieties are very hardcoated and soaking them usually produces almost 100% germination, and is a much safer and easier method than chipping the seed coat and possibly damaging the growing points.

Wednesday 20th   Up early to get the necessary chores in the house finished by the time Bill Lockerbie arrived at 8 a.m. He and David, the young forester, were to plant the ornamental trees and make some sort of guards to keep off deer, sheep, hares and rabbits. Left Brian filling the sweet pea trenches with manure and went up to the Langfield wood to find the others planting the walnuts; beautiful trees, three feet high, from Mr. Crane of Buxton. Jimmy Dey, the gamekeeper, was shooting remaining rabbits in the wood, some suffering from myximatosis, and some clean; so the trees may get more chance to grow safely.

February   During the rest of the day, in between four visitors being entertained to lunch, sowed sweet peas; Anne Vestey, Blue Triumph, Royal Flush, Knee-Hi, Majesty, Larkspur, Gaiety, Gertrude Tingay, and two packets of mixed varieties which are always interesting to grow. Some vegetable seeds were also sown.

Thursday 21st   It is Bob's 27th birthday today and fortunately still mild and springlike. The woodpecker was busy near the beck, and curlews were back on the damp ground down the park calling in the distance – that haunting, wonderful cry that turns my heart whenever I hear it. Birds were wakening around six-thirty outside my bedroom window; thrushes competing with robins to greet the first light, followed by a variety of little birds, particularly wrens who have found cosy hiding places where they could survive the storms. Curlews sometimes waken first, possibly disturbed by a fox trotting home before Jimmy can spy it on his early rounds. It is wonderful to see the dawn breaking once more as I open the heavy oak shutters in the ground floor rooms, barred each night against intruders, as they have been for generations past. The sun rising through the lacy branches of the beech trees lifts one's heart with joy at the certainty of spring days not far ahead.

Friday 22nd   Reg cut back some yew branches that had almost destroyed and buried a silver variegated holly bush on the edge of the Grove; they are such decorative trees, and now being so expensive to buy, one must encourage the ones already in the garden to grow. Lifted a few trumpet daffodils from enormous clumps which were growing in front of the roses and replanted them in bare patches in the Low Garden. Daffodils of many varieties are well up among the grass, while snowdrops and aconites are covering the bank with glory.

Catching endless poor mice with traps in the greenhouse on the soil warming bench. I'm afraid they may eat the seedlings and the sweet pea seeds. Put little heaps of mouse bait under broken flower pots in other corners in addition to the traps. It is sadly such a cosy retreat for these nice clean-coated country mice.

Saturday 23rd   *Huntfield.*   Back at Huntfield, and on turning the glass which was covering the seeds sown last Sunday, find the lettuces already through. Some old cyclamen corms are flowering remarkably well on the same bench. Tomato seedlings also through, coming evenly and strongly. I thought they might have needed more heat than the cable and the blower can provide, the latter only turned on from 5 p.m. till 9 a.m. to save electricity.

Sunday 24th   Davy here at last, after having spent several weekends helping to clear up fire damage which had gutted the tannery where he works in Lanark. He turned over a lot of ground and opened up the sweet pea trench. This is usually left open to the frost for some weeks.

February   I pruned roses on the walls outside the garden. Only last summer's growth was alive, the rabbits having gnawed the main trunks of the roses the previous winter. Since then a proper rabbit fence had been erected for it is on this border that all our vegetables are grown. I was very tired by nightfall.

Monday 25th   Slept badly. I must have pruned and tidied up for many hours during the weekend. Plums and apples growing against the somewhat low walls are to be allowed to have their heads in future so that they may develop and thereby fruit more effeciently instead of cutting them back annually.

Woodpigeons and rock doves coo-ing in the fir woods above the garden. How dull and frightening the world would be with no birds to sing and call.

Tuesday 26th   *Dalemain.*   Back to Dalemain, and a glorious run up Tweed. The colours in the little hanging valleys are so beautiful in the spring-like weather. The trees seemed to be stretching their slowly wakening branches up to the heights of the heavens. I wonder if it feels wonderful to be a tree, standing higher than everything around it, nearer to God and to Heaven; able to worship in the morning air, unsullied by the world of human beings. Perhaps it would be rather cold to be so tall and so very much alone.

Wednesday 27th   Went over to Ambleside to Hayes nursery gardens to try and find a Handker-chief tree, *Davidia involucrata*. Over the top of the Kirkstone Pass, out of a lovely day and into swirling mist on the southern side, and very cold down at Windermere. There are such well-grown shrubs and trees in the nursery garden, all expensive but beautifully produced. There were lovely Chinese witch-hazels costing £18; not long ago I bought them for £3 and £5 and thought that a big price, but everything has changed so much in the last few years. Found a beautiful *Davidia* costing £10 and looked in vain for *Acer aureum* to replace the magnificent specimen in the Low Garden which is dying back because it was planted in a part of the garden that floods when the Beck is high. Found an *Acer senkaki* which has lovely coral coloured bark, a variety that struggled for some years to grow at Huntfield, and eventually died. Such nice assistants, Patrick and Michael, who had worked at Hayes since leaving school. Finally they found an *Acer aureum* not long grafted on to a three foot stock of a common Japanese maple, costing £18, the most expensive tree I have ever bought. Patrick showed me the parent tree, the fine old *Acer aureum* growing in the garden from which they take cuttings, to be grafted by an expert. I must learn to do this sort of thing. My expensive purchase must be kept in a frost-free greenhouse for the present. A magnificent rose red azalea plant completed the purchases. Next week the prices were all going up and today there was 10% off purchases over £25, so I was lucky.

Mother and I picnicked half way up "The Struggle" overlooking the lake; it was so peaceful, scarcely a car on the road. She enjoyed these plant-hunting expeditions.

February
Friday 29th

Brian and I planted the precious trees in the Low Garden protecting each with rabbit netting; the *Davidia*, sometimes called the Dove or Ghost Tree, near the Beck as it should grow into a tall tree; the *Senkaki* under the bank sheltered by overhanging branches. I was advised to give the maples dried blood at times to feed and stimulate growth, and hope this treatment will encourage the older *Acer aureum* to put on some young growth and to recover. The replacement tree was put into a cool corner of the greenhouse for the present.

March
Saturday 1st

The weather is becoming colder, which is sad when frogs are croaking and spawning in the pond and toads are waking up and creeping down the steps into the Low Garden. I nearly stood on a terrified bright yellow chap who sat panting on a ledge at the bottom of the steps. Wrens flit about in the greenhouse where greenfly is in need of being destroyed.

When the days of splendour of the eighteenth and the first half of the nineteenth century had faded and times had become much harder, only part of the original Low Garden remained, the larger portion becoming meadow-land below the terrace walls. When I was a small child, the craze for Wild Gardens became the fashion, and Mother set about clearing snowberry and undergrowth from beneath the apple trees in the remaining part of that Garden. Sackloads of daffodils were planted, forsythia, cherry trees, and purple-leaved prunus were added to give colour in blossom time. Granny had planted a border of *Rhododendron ponticum* between the meadow and the orchard in 1911, and it was here in this secluded corner that Mother created her "Wild Garden" which gave her so much pleasure.

Because it was difficult to move the lawn mower down the steps into the "Wild Garden", Mother used a hand machine and frequently mowed the long grass paths herself. I remember her being utterly exhausted on many occasions, when it would have been so easy for the motor mower to have been driven down the park and across the Low Garden to cut her paths, which weaved their way in and out of the long grasses in summer time.

Father's older cousins, Dorothy and Eva also planted daffodils among the apple trees and some of these older varieties are still in evidence. It was here too, that these Victorian ladies created their water-colour paintings of the garden and elsewhere on the estate: they were born and brought up at Dalemain, which they loved dearly, and their water-colours and some early photographs are an interesting record at the turn of the century.

Sunday 2nd

Huntfield. Took a lot of cuttings of geraniums and fuschias and left the former to callous over till morning; this prevents them rotting, and should produce almost 100% success in rooting. Some of the geranium cuttings were of a variety called *Regina* purchased at the Highland Show. The original plant had been brought out of Austria by a nurseryman at the beginning of the war; it is a very beautiful variety.

Unless one can provide sufficient heat to induce autumn cuttings to root, it

March is safer to leave them growing on the old plants. Once the year has truly turned there is an urgency in the atmosphere which miraculously encourages even the weakest surviving plants to hang on to life and attempt to grow.

Monday 3rd *Anemone hepatica* is blooming well; some strong divisions of the older plants had been previously planted in other parts of the garden and were growing successfully. Such a beautiful plant with its starry powder-blue flowers. It likes the cool, deep, acid soil with a stone or two nearby to give it support and protection. A cloche helps to protect the delicate flowers which will bloom prolifically for many weeks, in the right conditions. Some day I must obtain the equally beautiful pink variety.

Tuesday 4th *Dalemain.* Took a mass of cuttings, geraniums, both woolly and ivy leaved; *ballota* and the silver-leaved *Helichrysum pettiolaris*. The cut surfaces of the geraniums were left to callous over for twenty-four hours as usual, but the others, including ivy-leaved varieties, were dipped into a rooting powder and lined out in a seed box in a sandy mixture. Another box was made ready for all sorts of cuttings that might be taken. The first were from the citrus which produces sweet-scented white flowers; little pieces of variegated ivies went in next.

Wednesday 5th Rachel Halsey, Bob's future mother-in-law, came to lunch and we toured the garden in the rain; she, robed in one of our old mackintoshes as it had been a lovely morning and quite unlike a shower. I do hope I do not bore our visitors, but it gives me such pleasure to wander round and gaze anew upon the plants and trees and to have time to look at something different on each garden tour. Perhaps my enthusiasm urges the poor visitors on; whether they are being polite or really interested is hard to tell as I find myself enthusing about something I had scarcely noticed previously.

One American friend later remarked that only an English lady gardener, so filled with enthusiasm, would take a visitor to look at her garden in the dusk!

Thursday 6th *Huntfield.* The *Viburnum fragrans*, Bodnant variety, has successfully layered itself twice over, even though it is an upright shrub. Cut the branch carefully and dug up the well rooted portions which had already become quite shrubs in their own right. Transplanted one near to the house where we can enjoy its beauty more regularly, and wrapped the second one up to plant in the Wild Garden at Dalemain. The parent shrub has flowered since November and even after a wintry spell it has refreshed itself and looks as perfect as ever, even at 1,000 feet above sea level.

Friday 7th Went down to Heavyside where the Gibson family farm. It is in rich land, once part of the Biggar bog which was drained long ago. Here the old-fashioned purple crocuses seed all down the wooded drive, and a thick purple carpet covers the rough grass beneath the widely spaced trees like a film of blue in the evening light. They seed freely on to the edge of the drive in great clumps, which become spoiled with weedkiller in the summer, so my friend Mrs. Gibson said she would dig some of these up for Huntfield and also for Dalemain. The strange part is that aconites I have given her in the past fail to spread in that lovely dark soil which is very similar to the peaty soil at Huntfield. In the meantime, she gave me a bag of sprouting corms which she had put aside in the house a long time ago; so these were hastily planted in the gravel by out kitchen door.

Sunday 9th Marita and Mrs. Gibson arrived in the evening with two cartons filled with clumps of crocuses – what a gorgeous present, and how I will enjoy planting them.

Monday 10th Moles are working hard; the grass up the garden is becoming patterned with their nice rich brown hills of newly thrown-up earth – so good for potting mixtures, but how to catch the moles! A writer of long ago suggests putting a live mole into "a deep earthenware potte set into the edge of the earth". When the poor mole realises it is enclosed it cries out and all the moles in the vicinity come to the rescue and fall into the "deep potte". But there are worse and more modern methods of dealing with the small black velvet-coated gentlemen. How sad that these little creatures are such a nuisance, but they have their uses too, and aerate the earth through their tunnelling.

Tuesday 11th Went to a funeral in Skirling church. Denis Wheeler-Carmichael was laid to rest among the snowdrops in a charming tiny churchyard with an enormous sycamore tree spreading its branches overhead. What a lovely place to lie, so sheltered and with the lambs bleating on the other side of the kirkyard wall.
   Dalemain. We went on to Dalemain, and looked at all the seeds, some small ones still protected by the propagator tops. Tiny calceolarias are still safe and growing well, and lobelia just through, so I removed the dark paper. Two boxes of sweet peas were moved to the small cold house, later to be filled with tomatoes; this made room for dahlia tubers boxed up last week, from which cuttings will be taken in due course. The sweet peas have germinated almost 100% and so evenly – really exciting; heliotrope looks quite strong, and antirrhinums also.
   Walked round the "Low Garden" and gazed upon the snowdrops drifting down the bank everywhere like white angels about to run down the hill to dance in the gathering dusk.

Wednesday 12th Planted Mrs. Gibson's crocuses up the drive edge alongside the Grove, so they will get shelter and sunshine all the year, and it is good dry ground for them to seed and overspill on to the gravel. Planted a few in a circle round the

| March | clipped box trees near the house where larger varieties seem to be taking hold at last; the birds and the mice give them little chance to multiply. |

Thursday 13th The most glorious morning after a sharp frost. It was so light when I rose at 6.30 a.m. that no light was needed. Sunlight filled the Grove and made the aconites shine like gold and gave a radiance to the carpet of snowdrops. Even the undersides of the leaves of the holly trees shone until their dark surfaces lit up and looked the colour of primroses. It was a truly wonderful morning; the birds so happy, and singing as if they would fill the whole world with songs.

Planted the *Viburnum bodnantense* in the Low Garden at the bottom of the bank where its precocious flowers will get shelter from overhanging trees.

Friday 14th Autumn crocuses, the meadow saffrons, are pushing up quantities of green leaves beneath the semi-wild shrubby spireas; they need to be moved since they get little sun. Dug up quite a number of clumps, but their tall green shoots needed careful handling in case they snapped off. Divided and replanted them round prunus trees along the path edge and in other sheltered corners.

Saturday 15th All the seedlings in the greenhouse are good and even. No failures so far. Tomatoes are ready to be either pricked out into boxes or potted on. Nipped the growing points out of all sweet peas that showed two open pairs of leaves so that they will grow into nice bushy, short-jointed plants.

Sunday 16th *Huntfield.* Back at Huntfield: Davy came and lifted the thick row of yew tree plantlets. These were cuttings inserted in a trench of sandy soil in Ted's old garden near the frames eighteen months ago. Last winter the rabbits nibbled them sorely, but they made enormous roots instead of top growth: when replanted they almost completed the circle of yews round the little statue in the Wild Garden. It pays over and over again to take cuttings of many plants and shrubs, so long as one is prepared to wait patiently. Yew trees to buy cost about £7 each and the circle would need about thirty-two plants, impossibly expensive to buy. I must root a further supply for future use.

Monday 17th When I rose, to my horror, it was snowing and everything was white; the trees and bushes looked like midwinter. Our little road was snowy, but the main roads were clear.

Dalemain. Set off for Dalemain with the car loaded with young silver birch trees about 2′6″ tall, lifted with nice peaty balls and with some heather attached to their roots. They grow like weeds at Huntfield and the reverse at Dalemain. Also with us went two well grown sweet-smelling poplars grown from cuttings. They root so easily and make lovely trees. These had originally come from cuttings off cuttings taken from my father-in-law's trees at

March   Southernwood, a house built at the turn of the century in the park of old Barnton House just outside Edinburgh. The owner of each house built in that park was bound by agreement to plant a holly hedge down their part of the avenue, which looks most attractive. Behind the holly hedge a line of these poplars had been planted to give more privacy.

Tuesday 18th   David, the forester, and I took the silver birches to plant in Grandiscar. We laid them out in groups of five or six to shine above the river when they grow older, and some along the field fence. The poplars were planted near the Deer Park wall so that their scent will be wafted towards the house in spring. Grandiscar is an Icelandic name meaning a strip of brightness along the edge of a dark hillside. Cumbria was settled by the Norsemen in the long ago days, and so the river Eamont at this point must have looked to these fierce people as a bright ribbon of water among the primeval forest that grew on the hillside above.

Wednesday 19th   Divided some good delphiniums, replanting the pieces to fill up the border behind the frames. They grow well in this border sheltered by the old brick walls and make a beautiful show. Any shoots that broke off were dipped into rooting powder and potted up in the greenhouse. The lovely variety "Strawberry Fair" divided into four nice pieces. We forked and cleaned the border before mulching with manure, and scattered "Slug Death" pellets to preserve the juicy shoots.

The bearded iris and polyanthus growing in front of the delphiniums are dreadful for harbouring the little annual willow herb and shepherd's purse, and need constant eradicating.

Thursday 20th   The dawn chorus begins around 5.30 a.m. I try and wake in order to listen to the first thrilling notes of the thrush on the holly tree with the knowledge that there is still time to lie abed and dream and think. Peewits call from their feeding grounds and a pair of mallard rise noisily from the rushes on the river edge and call as they fly upstream. Later in the day watched a heron standing, gaunt and shrivelled, near the ponies who were eating hay in the paddock beside the old dam.

It was still cold, but possible to plant a pair of beautiful golden yew trees, the Noah's Ark variety which will not grow more than five feet tall which Mother had given to me for a Christmas present. The snow was rapidly disappearing and the greater spotted woodpecker could be heard clearly, drumming away on a dying elm tree in the Deer Park, just behind the summer house. I could hear him at his work all the time while planting the yews which are to be a "gateway" on either side of a small flagged path at the top of the garden. They made it look more important. Little blue squills were bursting into flower at the foot of the two Lombardy cherries, *Prunus amanogawa*, the

March small columnar tree which produces dense upright clusters of fragrant shell pink flowers.

MARCH EVENING

Oh, ye mortals, stand and listen,
Listen to the surge of spring;
Be ye still and be ye silent,
Hear the news the tree tops bring.

See those gnarled and ancient beech trees,
Standing, waiting, watching still;
Cradled soft in moving moor mist
While their sleeping branches fill —

Fill with throbbing new-born magic,
Rushing sap and boundless joy;
Silent, silhouetted branches
Wait, impatient, fret, annoy.

Slow the lengthening shadows gather,
A thrush pours forth her sweetest song;
Her prayer of thankful praise and glory
For spring, for which all creatures long.

Forgotten all the winter sadness
Which fragile birds find hard to bear;
There only is the Great Tomorrow,
The healing sun, the softer air.

Written while waiting for Celandine and Harebell to eat their evening feed. These woolly-coated Fell Ponies had wintered well on our high lying ground with plenty of hay and a small nourishing feed each day to keep them warm. Celandine, my dearest pony, had brought fame and fun to the little herd. Her old mother, Heather, will soon be teaching little David and Saya something of the art of horsemanship. They will be able to sit on her back safely, and learn "to ride".

Friday 21st Finished putting cuttings of geraniums into sandy boxes. It was very cold, so nice to be working behind glass.

In the evening spoke to the Pooley Bridge W.I. My talk was called "Living Between Two Gardens" and I showed a film of the garden and the river taken in the snow and the frosty sunlight on New Year's Day, and of the aconites and cherry blooming cheerily only a few weeks later. Everyone seemed to enjoy the evening and asked lots of questions, making the gathering worthwhile.

Saturday 22nd *Huntfield.* Back at Huntfield where it was so cold and not encouraging to go outside. Snow had been lying quite thickly since Monday. It was so sad for the snowdrops, peeping over their white blanket rather droopily. Some of the

March　handsome bulbs called Snowflakes are in bloom, and the *Anemone hepatica* continues to flower under a cloche.

Sunday 23rd　Sowed some more cauliflower and lettuce seeds, and pricked out more tomato seedlings. The box of Greyhound cabbage which had been hardened off in the cold greenhouse looked touched with frost, but some of these were fit to prick out. One notices how quickly seedlings surge ahead as soon as they have been given a shift into a fresh mixture.

Despite the snow, the curlew were in full song away up at the top of the fields that border the hill and the heather, their haunting melody drifting down to the house. I thought I heard a skylark rising up into the heavens. Other little birds were very busy at their breakfast table outside the kitchen door. Even jackdaws alighted hungrily and flew back noisily to their nesting sites in disused chimney pots.

Monday 24th　*Dalemain.*　Seed boxes sown with coloured Cowslips and the old fashioned yellow varieties are coming through in multitudes – how exciting. We *must* preserve the wild flowers and their hybrids: all being well these seedlings will be pricked out in a frame or a sheltered place where they will stay until next spring. They should be planted in drifts in the grass to look natural, where they they can seed and repopulate the meadows.

In these days of fertilizers and ploughing up of so much marginal land for reseeding and to make better pastures for beef cattle, many wild flowers are becoming extremely rare. "The Divisions" beyond the top of Dacre Banks on the higher ground above the park at Dalemain, is, to me, a sad example of loss of natural herbage and the many varieties of unusual or local flowers that grew and seeded unhindered until these last years. This hundred and fifty acres was partly rushy and partly good land, once having been a small farm in the days gone by. That exquisite grey-veined buttercup-shaped flower of the white Grass of Parnassus grew profusely; butterfly, marsh and spotted orchis's seeded in the damp places; butterworts, milkworts and valerians grew prolifically; the little yellow rosettes of the leaves of the butterworts shone in the sunshine, their pointed tips and curled edges appearing to a child to be like tiny hats of the fairy people who must have haunted these beautiful acres. The most exquisite flower of all was the Bird's Eye primrose – *Primula farinosa* – which grew everywhere, their rosy, lilac flowerets dusted with soft velvet-like farina. Not far away to the northwest, Blencathra, Carrock, and the other Mungrisedale fells rise majestically above the boggy ground that stretches far away towards Hesket Newmarket and John Peel's country.

The "Green Lane" bordering the Divisions on the east side was a dirt road till the 'fifties when the County Council and their tarmacadam caused the disappearance of yet more precious flowers. A large bed of the yellow Herb Paris grew luxuriantly beneath the shelter of willows, hazels and other self-regenerated trees. The single line railway track to Keswick crossing the Divisions was a haven for primroses, violets and other wild flowers, besides

March being a dry and cosy place along the railway banks for birds to nest. A corncrake nested in a hole in the underpass of the railway, and now these birds are rare. There are still a few places on the Divisions where the wild flowers can grow, if only the fertilizers do not destroy those that remain; the disused railway embankment at least, is a sanctuary and cannot be ploughed out!

Tuesday 25th Motored over the Devil's Beef Tub where great drifts of snow lay at the sides of the road, and the lines of Christmas trees planted interminably across the hills stood out like soldiers upon the whitened ground.

Further down the road it was a beautiful day, and at Dalemain Bill Lockerbie was planting two *Cedrus atlantica* in the park. These trees were presented to us by the staff of the estate and the household to mark the celebrations held last summer when our family had lived at Dalemain for three hundred years. These green cedars were suggested as a suitable present which would stand the years of time. The Cedars of Lebanon which we had hoped to plant seemed to be unobtainable, but shortly may be available as very small trees; however, the green Atlantic Cedars should look equally beautiful. They too were hard to find, many nurseries only growing the grey-needled variety, *glauca*, which we have already planted in various places.

Wednesday 26th The most perfect day of the year. Brian planted five long rows of Jerusalem artichokes, using about three buckets full of seed to do so; the remainder will be used to eat or to be sold when the house opens at Easter in a week's time. They are such a useful winter vegetable and also make delicious soup. Much tidying up to be done before that date; the drive needs to be raked and cleaned while some of the variegated thuyas, boxwood and hollies require to be clipped back. Some of these were planted by Stuart and Bill Slee about fifty years ago when I was a very small girl; I remember so well watching them digging and planting. Nothing which Stuart planted ever failed to grow, but one of his secrets of success would be to see that the ground was properly prepared beforehand, so that whatever was planted could stand the march of time.

Friday 28th *Iris reticulata* coming into flower in many places. These small stately iris's seem to be targets for the birds and yet some of them survive to multiply into clumps. For many, many years they have bloomed under musk roses – that lovely creamy pink variety called Penelope, which grow in a narrow well-drained border alongside the remains of the old greenhouse; the walls, built with lime mortar are ideal and seem to give them immunity from pests. A few rock tulips continue in the same manner on the terrace border where drainage is perfect. In the wild, these spring bulbs grow in mountainous areas where the sun bakes their bulbs in summertime. Whenever one plants, particularly bulbs and lilies, one must think of the natural habitat of these treasures, and being so expensive to buy nowadays, they must be given the most ideal conditions possible.

Sunday 30th *Huntfield.* Bryce's 60th birthday, an auspicious occasion, so I put a posy of heathers and little sprays of hemlock spruce on our breakfast table. The heathers are a boon to colour the spring garden at this high altitude, never failing to flower. Springwood White and Springwood Pink and some other varieties are a mass of bloom giving shelter to early bulbs and dwarf rhododendrons besides protecting them from hungry birds. So long as heathers are given a light shearing after flowering to prevent them becoming woody and untidy they are unfailingly beautiful.

Planted out three boxes of hyacinth bulbs. These arrived during a hard spell, and rather than leave them in a bag to sprout, they were planted in seedboxes which were set under a lilac tree in the garden. By this method they seemed to have survived attacks from mice and other pests and were sprouting happily as I planted them in various places near the pool.

Frogs were busy in the pool and the spawn was already there in thick jellied masses. Elderly frogs were making extraordinary deep bull-like noises as they happily played about among the water weeds, peeping up now and again to see what was going on in the world beyond the water.

April Went to Glasgow to visit a cousin in hospital. The crocuses along the "Clyde *Tuesday 1st* Expressway" were absolutely beautiful, and again in Carluke they were growing profusely. This goes to prove that the dirt and soot from built-up areas protects crocuses against mice and slugs, or how else do they multiply so wonderfully?

Mrs. Gibson's old-fashioned crocuses which were planted in the gravel on the path leading to the garden are already eaten down, when I was hoping so much that their seeds would ripen and germinate. So far, the ones planted in the garden are untouched.

Wednesday 2nd *Dalemain.* Everyone was busy tidying up at Dalemain, for the house and garden would be open to the public from Easter Saturday till October. There was an air of intense activity as the cobbled courtyard was swept clean, the drive edged and swept, the gravel paths in the garden raked, while the lawns had their first cut of the season. They looked so nice and smooth like velvet with the pile laid back in long tram lines. If the house was not open to visitors it would be quite impossible to keep it up, and the whole place would quickly fall into disrepair. As it is, there is an air of eager expectancy, for a house like Dalemain needs people, and children to be around. Historic houses were never built to be museums; they were always a centre for the community of the neighbourhood, and in the early days a place of refuge, especially in the "Debatable Lands" of the Border country.

Spent the entire morning arranging vases of greenery, half-opened flowering currant and forsythia, all round the house. There were sprays of larch dotted with green furls of half-opened buds, shiny-leaved mahonia, thuya, both gold and green, hemlock spruce with graceful silvered reverse sides to its branches; ivy with tiny green snowballs for flower-heads, and a few treasures such as *Viburnum fragrans* and variegated ivy to lend interest to the arrangements. Jean, who has helped me at Huntfield since the boys were small, gave me a present of a beautiful bouquet of spray carnations for Easter and these looked lovely in the drawing rooms and in the Old Oak room, mixed with suitable greeneries to fill the flower vases; heathers and a few precious daffodils were gathered somewhat reluctantly to make a splash of colour in Uncle Godfrey's bedroom which now displays silver, dresses, Victorian children's clothes, High Sheriffs' banners, photographs and little treasures.

Saturday 5th The house opened its doors to the visitors for the fourth season; how they enjoy to gaze at everything and to wonder how anyone could live in such a vast place; one hears such remarks from time to time – "do they *really* live here?"

Sunday 6th Easter Day.   Dacre Church was dressed in all the glory of springtime with daffodils and forsythia proclaiming the Message that the Lord has risen indeed. The resurrection of the spring returns and with it the certainty that we too shall be reborn. Year after year we wait expectantly for the earth's awakening; we never doubt the return of the spring, this annual miracle which we so often take for granted. So, why should we doubt the resurrection of our spiritual bodies? We sing with such fervour "Jesus Christ is risen today" and are deeply happy to be able to share in His triumph. If it were not true, we could not possibly feel so elated.

Monday 7th Over two hundred visitors today; considerably more than on this date last year. Managed to prune roses in the garden while talking to some of them. It is difficult to work and look respectable at the same time: the visitors are always anxious to talk and ask questions, and one can sometimes learn something new from these conversations.

In the mornings of late, managed to find time to pot up plants for the sales stall. Aconites need to be potted at this season for in a little while they will completely disappear and though they grow profusely in various places they will be impossible to find once they have died down. At the moment they are setting quantities of seed, and already thousands of seedlings have sprouted up from last year's crop. They appear in the gravel and among leafy places, wherever these heralds of spring can manage to establish themselves.

The greenhouse is filled with pans and boxes of seedlings, many pricked out already; sweet peas have been moved into a cold frame alongside cauliflower

April   seedlings, and others, to harden off and make room for fresh sowings in the greenhouse.

Wednesday 9th   *Huntfield.*   Brian has flu which is somewhat of a worry as we returned to Huntfield leaving the greenhouses in a precarious situation with only Bob or Jack Holliday (who helps in the Estate Office) to open, shut and water when they have time, or when they can remember. Living in two places is very difficult and often dreadfully exasperating especially where plant life is concerned.

   The boxes of seed potatoes, all sprouting, are waiting anxiously to be planted – perhaps next week.

Thursday 10th   The seed pan of *Begonia semperflorens* arrived safely from Dobbies of Chester, filled to overflowing with well-grown seedlings. After being carefully watered, these were placed inside a larger seed pan, covered with a propagator top, and set in the greenhouse in a warm, moist atmosphere where they soon began to revive after their journey. Last year I managed to prick out about five hundred seedlings from the same sized pan, though some were very tiny and not all survived. Some of the ensuing plants were potted up last autumn and are now looking well, ready to decorate the house; others have had cuttings removed from them which will eventually grow into good plants.

Friday 11th   Last Friday, being Good Friday, was the most glorious warm sunny day, but as on so many Good Fridays the sun became dimmed with clouds about mid-day, the sky remaining overcast until about 4 p.m. For many years this clouding of the sun has been most noticeable, and whether it is a phenomenon or not, the whole earth seems to remember Our Lord's suffering.

   Flowering shrubs in Edinburgh are already a glorious sight. Pale pink pyrus blossom in St. Andrew's Square on low-growing umbrella-shaped trees is a sight for tired eyes. The gardens throughout this splendid city have long since been renowned; being almost at sea-level, there is always something of interest in bloom.

Saturday 12th   The little bulbs take over in the garden at this season of the year. *Chionodoxa luciliae*, the Glory of the Snow, is one of the most perfect, seeding itself inprofusion in beds that are not overworked and are rich in humus. Their sky-blue faces turned Heavenwards, their white centres setting off the blue. Sky-blue scillas too, squills as we called them long ago, and still *Anemone hepaticas* continue to bloom.

Sunday 13th   Barley is being sown during this dry spell. Tractors humming away in every direction – "The better the day, the better the deed." Much of our barley is being put in by a contractor, so perhaps as it is the Sabbath we will be blessed with a good crop. Flocks of rooks are in evidence alighting on the newly-

April worked soil in search of wire worms. Grandfather maintained that rooks were the farmer's best friend, and that the rookeries round the farm steadings should never be shot or disturbed.

Monday 14th Gentle rain fell in the early morning and the fields glisten with that gorgeous soft green look when grasses semed to have jumped an inch overnight. A pair of oyster-catchers flew overhead calling that magical call as they made their way to the marshy ground along the Clyde. Curlews spread their wide wings, half hesitating in mid-air before diving warily in to the middle of a field where they are probably nesting. Greenfinches abound in the shrubs, and bullfinches are already hopping along the garden walls behind the blackcurrant bushes in search of grubs.

Tuesday 15th Another lovely day, warm and sunny after the small amount of rain yesterday. Pruned roses which were planted last autumn and forked and hoed the beds. Neither tea nor floribunda roses are at all reliable at this height, and by the time the dead wood was cut away, there was frequently little of the rose to be seen. In spite of looking so sparse at this moment, it is wonderful how they will bloom so well by mid-summer.

Wednesday 16th *Dalemain.* Journeyed back to Dalemain with seedlings in boxes ready to be pricked out either to sell at a later date or to be bedded out. A box of yellow doronicums went too; these grow almost wild in the grass at Huntfield and revel in the moist peaty conditions, so they might take hold and spread when planted in the Low Garden.

Ted arrived from Paris where he is painting at Les Beaux Artes, and we walked into Lobb's Wood together: it is looking more of a fairy-like wood than ever with cosy clumps of primroses tucked up comfortably beneath the young beech trees, and against old tree roots on the bank where a hedge must have grown in the past.

Thursday 17th It is amazing how seedlings appear of both plants and trees and frequently flourish much more easily than carefully planted specimens. Three good young Douglas Firs have settled themselves in Lobb's Wood. Seeds must have been carried by birds from the huge trees we cut over a year ago in the Low Garden. They had been planted by Father in 1910 and grew to an enormous height and girth, completely overshadowing everything and even darkening the walled garden above; yet their gracful branches seemed to garland the house and the terrace as if they were in a picture frame, when one was walking near the Dacre Beck. They were cut one frosty December morning, and my heart was in my mouth as each thud pronounced the death of a tree; the second morning it rained incessantly, and the tractors cut deeper into the daffodils as they dragged the massive boles over the bank where the Victorian clumps of these bulbs still flourish. When spring returned one could scarcely

April   realize that this tall colony of Douglas Firs had ever existed. The grass has knitted together, and somehow, the old pheasant's-eye narcissi have renewed their strength in their search for sunlight, flowering as they have not done for a long time when they were overshadowed by the vast Douglas Firs.

Sunday 20th   *Huntfield.*   Clear starry nights as the frost gathers and moves down the hill, following the burn, frequently missing the garden at Huntfield as it moves like a ghost with flow of water. Venus shines brightly and seems to be incredibly near the earth. These are dangerous days for gardeners; greenhouses becoming much too hot by day and the temperature dropping sharply at night. One must damp down after mid-day to keep that lovely growy atmosphere, allowing time for the greenhouse to become drier before dusk.

Monday 21st   Some of the Agapanthus in large pots are in need of repotting and dividing. Some of these will divide into a dozen or more plants. Eventually some of the undisturbed pots of flowering agapanthus will stand round the pool, while the young ones will be ready to sell to the tourists. Their long tangled succulent roots soon settle down into a mixture rich in leaf-mould and sharp sand, with a little old rotted manure and moss above the crocks. The closed atmosphere of the greenhouse encourages growth before they stand outside in early June when all fear of frost is past.

     Gentian acaulis are soon to make a wonderful show at Huntfield. They are such temperamental plants, but if they like their situation they thrive. One clump continues to bloom profusely from a corner in the rock walk. A few years ago I tried to split it up and nearly lost all the tiny plantlets, but it recovered and is now a cushion of buds. This variety likes to grow in a cool, sunny position.

Thursday 24th   *Daphne mezereon* in full bloom, scenting the air as one passes. Such strange plants; they flower for many years and then with no warning depart this life and no one seems to know the reason. With any luck they set seeds, or at least birds drop them here and there. I am always on the lookout for seedlings of any sort which may need a little cosseting; as a result there have been many generations of the original Daphne growing in our gardens. I always mean to collect the seed as it ripens and sow some in a box, but invariably the birds have devoured the brilliant red berries all too quickly.

Friday 25th   *Daphne retusa* is even more lovely and grows on the north side of the garden wall facing the house. Bought originally in three inch pots from a rock nursery in Barrhead about thirty years ago when we were newly married, they have moved wherever we have lived and scented the air most beautifully. As they grow and spread, more leaf-mould is worked in among their splaying branches. Cuttings root very easily, and a few of these are growing well at Dalemain in quite a different soil. Snow frequently spreads and frays the branches with its weight, but with a little more leaf-mould they partially layer themselves, thus growing even more profusely.

Saturday 26th   *Dalemain.*   Woke up to a sharp white frost. The soft green shoots of the delphiniums were turned over looking quite lifeless, but by mid-morning they appeared unharmed.

The Low Garden, which Mother called her Wild Garden, is like a dream with all the white narcissi taking over from the deeper yellows of earlier weeks. Overhanging these are crowds of "garden party ladies", – the white damson blossom, its dark blackish bark standing out starkly against the snowy flowers below.

Pricked out boxes of seedlings most of which have come up like mustard and cress this year. What a time-consuming occupation, but using the top of a frame as a bench in the sunshine, it was no penance to fill box after box while visitors passed the time of day and talked.

Monday 28th   A little shower blew from the lake now and again, but the earth has become so dry that it made no impression. Every frame needs steady watering, and the greenhouses much spraying to keep that lovely warm, moist growy atmosphere, so vital to plant life.

Pruned a large area of roses. Many of the red ones were presents from the family to Mother and Father for their Ruby Wedding in 1960. They are tremendously strong, healthy twenty year olds, varieties like Frensham, Baccara, Super Star, and the rich scented Madame Louise Laperrière, and none have been replaced. How strange that on some bushes the bursting shoots have been frosted while on neighbouring bushes they were unscathed.

Took the long top shoots as cutings from Mrs. James Laing, that gorgeous, scented cabbagey pink rose, and moved young bushes of Celestial which grow so readily, to a nursery bed. Some are already for sale. The sunset yellow Alchemist is another shrub rose which grows well from cuttings and the floppy pink Constance Spry likewise. The majority of these and other cuttings, well-buried in a sandy trench, will root; in these expensive days it is the best way to stock a garden.

Wednesday 30th   "Fill the waking world with glory . . ." so wrote Frances Ridley Havergal a hundred and fifty years ago, and this was just how I felt when waking with the birds and their Dawn Chorus before 5 a.m. How true those same words ring when song thrushes and blackbirds sit in the holly trees close to my bedroom window, and pour forth such jubilant melodies that it really is impossible not to wake. Water hens croak happily across the meadow from the Eamont, and curlews hover, dive and call down the park with the first light. It is so much easier to rise from a downy couch when daylight comes early. Sometimes I take a bucket of ashes from the wood fire down the garden and sprinkle it close to delphiniums and other delectable plants to help to ward off slugs. By

April the time the ashes are on the ground they are quite cool, and since this is a very economical source of potash, it is wasteful to put it in the ash bin which is eventually carted up the Church road, its contents used to fill potholes which become so much worse in these days when tractors race along estate roads. These early morning sallies down the terrace renew one's strength; the earth takes on that glorious gown of greenery and refreshment as the light mists lift off the Ullswater valley and quickly disappear into thin air. Each tiny flower in the border and every spear of tulip leaves pushing upwards from the good rich earth takes on another hue. So many people miss the wonders of the dawning when they lie in bed too long.

Brian and I worked at the long terrace border as the sun rose higher in the heavens, forking and weeding and cutting away dead wood among the roses. The birds were busy everywhere and young lambs frolicked in along the uneven edges of the beck sides. We decided that success in life is not making "a go" in the business world, nor rushing about in a social world; true success is peace of mind and the tranquility one absorbs from working in a garden.

May
Thursday 1st The dry cold wind returned and at this season it is called the Blackthorn Winter; it is well named with all its untimely persistence. The Helm Wind lies over the East Fells, while the white blossom cloaks the bare dark-stemmed twigs of the black-thorn bushes that grow profusely in Grandiscar along the water's edge and in so many hedges and coppices in Cumbria. It is from its berries that sloe gin is made and very potent this liquor can be. Invariably at this time of year the ground is dried out with cold harsh winds and it is madness to try and "plant out", even the sweet peas, which are now properly hardened off.

Cleaned the long shrub rose border that slopes fairly steeply downhill to the greenhouses. The border was well manured during the winter, much of which lay as a mulch round the rose bushes protecting them against the drying winds.

The hoe really is the gardener's best friend. The ground is too dry to fork and anyhow it is too hard work for my poor back which gives trouble at times; but one can hoe carefully and uproot the willow herbs, tufts of grass and creeping buttercups.

Sunday 4th One should never leave to do tomorrow what one can do today, and the longer one gardens all the year round, the more apparent it becomes; one can never catch up. Spring is always in a hurry. The earth feels full of excitement and that tremendous urge of resurrection. So often one wishes that those magic moments would stand still just a little while. Before long it will be midsummer, and autumn will be upon us; springtime is newborn and wonderful in the same way that little children are so beautiful. Their eyes are clear and enquiring, their tiny hands and feet smooth and untarnished with hard work and too much use.

A bag of *Galtonia* bulbs, the tall white Cape hyacinths, arrived a month ago,

May and being in a hurry with no time to plant them in the garden I buried them in a deep seed box and left them outside near the frames. Today they were planted in the old vine border in front of the greenhouse. They were growing fast with tentacles of roots already in operation. What a good thing they were allowed to grow instead of shrivelling in a paper bag.

Monday 5th Heard the chiff-chaff calling up in Friarsdarrock; such a lovely song of springtime and warm days, but still the Helm Wind sears the ground and heavy black banks of clouds lie solid over the East Fells.

As I hoed in the shelter of the yew trees at the top of the garden, a pair of chaffinches preened themselves on the Wild Garden wall behind me, taking no notice of my nearness. The little hen puffed herself up and sat watching her mate as he danced backwards and forwards, sweeping his tail this way and that like a brush upon the wall top. This love dance went on for ages; they were quite enchanting to watch, and so beautiful.

Meanwhile goldfinches were flying about among the apple blossom, the gold in their wings shining suddenly as they darted from tree to tree. If a little hoeing can be done each day in this dry weather, the weeds may be kept in check.

Arum Lilies are coming into flower in the greenhouse. I am not always very successful with these Easter lilies, probably from lack of heat in winter time, but this year even the young ones in five inch pots are putting up flowers. All the greenhouse plants were fed lately with a pinch of sulphate of potash to each pot after which it was well watered in, so perhaps this is the reason they look well and solid at this time. Arum lilies in particular enjoy good clean chopped turves in their potting mixture, and it is very handy to have a pile of these handy, especially for an inside job in bad weather.

Thursday 8th At last the sweet peas were planted out. The nights are still quite cold with sharp frost and brilliant stars, but the days grow hotter as the month passes. Already the ground is like dust though quite damp underneath, but it would be hopeless to plant out any tender plants in these conditions. The sweet peas were protected with spruce branches on both sides of the wire netting and well watered in. They had been well hardened off in a cold frame for the past weeks.

Friday 9th *Huntfield.* Back at Huntfield, and planted the sweet peas there; the complete difference in the atmosphere and in the texture of the peaty soil makes planting a less anxious procedure. The winds are still cold from the snow-capped hills, but with a goodly "hedge" of *Abies grandis* branches growing nearby and easy to cut, they were well protected. It is really a pleasure to plant out in this soil which never dries out.

Pricked out more seedlings into boxes – scented tobacco plants, mesembryanthemums, dianthus and violas. I have come to the conclusion that one

May   must plant and divide more perennial flowers and grow biennials which can become established in their flowering quarters in October/November, or planted in the early spring, thus avoiding the trouble of planting in dry weather at a later date.

Paeonies are looking well with a mulch of strawy manure packed round their tubers, their plum-coloured foliage making a perfect foil for tulips flowering amongst them. These tulips remain *in situ* and develop into clusters instead of being lifted and stored where they would be eaten by mice.

Monday 12th   Put pig netting guards over the delphiniums. Any left-over lengths of fencing wire are collected and cut into suitable lengths. These are afterwards moved on to later flowering perennials. With a firm stake or two to prevent them blowing over, such guards are most useful and save much tying and staking in the early stages. Tall stakes are added to support the delphiniums when they grow above the circle of wire.

Tuesday 13th   *Dalemain.*   The heat is becoming aggressive. It is at least six weeks since there was rain at Dalemain, though Huntfield has had an occasional shower. The ground is developing cracks where it has been left bare; it is even difficult to keep the frames cool since the old yew trees, which once shaded them at a distance, were cut back to their original hedge status.

Wednesday 14th   Potted up a variety of perennials for the stall, assisted by Pam and Helen who came to assist me from the village nearby which was a wonderful help. I dug up plants which they planted in containers using a good mixture which we had in readiness. We potted up clusters of aconites too since the visitors frequently ask for them, and once they have died down they are impossible to find even though the Grove is full of them. *Rosa rubrifolia* seeds itself generously, and young plants of this dark-leaved shrub rose were potted up in readiness for the stall. When the old bushes are garlanded with deep red hips they are a beautiful sight and very useful for floral art.

The apple green Corsican Hellebore have produced quite a number of seedlings. These must be cosseted for future use; when the sun shines on their heavy clusters of flower heads they are a beautiful sight – they look particularly lovely when grown on a slope.

Thursday 15th   The blossom is quite wonderful. Usually at 1,000 feet up it is uncertain and not particularly profuse, but with the drought and hot sun forcing the buds into flower, weeping cherries and other varieties are like a dream of Heaven against the clear blue sky. Varieties of narcissi are quite startling in the heat of the day, particularly the beautiful double White Lion, and Mrs. Backhouse (which is the original "pink daffodil"), or pure white Actea, and many others.

For many years, after moving to Huntfield, I bought a few bulbs of newer varieties each autumn, and these have multiplied in the good dark soil. These

May bulbs were always planted in beds among shrub roses or other perennials, so that they could be lifted easily and divided after a few years had elapsed. When planted in grass they are much more difficult to lift. In this way, many newer varieties have populated both gardens.

One of the loveliest of the smaller daffodils is called "Doves' Wings"; their white sepals curve backwards in the way that cyclamen grow and look their best at this time of year when the garden is open in aid of District Nurses under Scotland's Garden Scheme. Usually when we open, half the proceeds are given to the Thistle Foundation, the village founded originally for disabled ex-servicemen and their families at Craigmillar, on the outskirts of Edinburgh.

Friday 16th *Huntfield.* The heat is quite devastating – it is impossible to work in the walled garden during the middle of the day. By tea-time, the primroses which have grown for years amongst the roots of the Celestial Roses, looked almost withered and dead. I have never seen anything like it at this time of year when everything is struggling to put on growth.

The Huntfield garden having been liberally manured for many years and copiously covered with leaf-mould into the bargain is usually a splendid seed bed for the primula family, but this year is exceptional and some of them are struggling to survive. The tomato coloured candelabra primula "Inverewe" is coming into bloom; the three original plants have multiplied into dozens of plants. A goodly bed near the pool has a cool root run against a low north-facing wall and there they make a wonderful display. Other candelabra primulas are also coming into bloom, pinks, yellows and all shades of claret and mauve; the moonlight primula, *Alpicola*, which smells deliciously, grows in the shade behind the garden wall, while the yellow heladoxa, the Himalayan Cowslip, makes a handsome corner close to a huge old philadelphus.

At this time of year every corner of the garden or the woodlands has something exciting and different to look upon. Perhaps the loveliest are the elm trees covered with primrose-coloured flowers which light up like gossamer when the soft sunlight shines upon them. How sad to see the elm trees further south stricken by the Dutch Elm disease. So far Huntfield has escaped, but Dalemain which has many ancient elm trees, has become affected. People think I am mad to go on planting small elm trees, but possibly when these grow older they will have become immunized.

Saturday 17th Watched fascinated from the drawing room window while a hen blackbird carefully acquired a large dried flower head of *Sedum spectablis* and carried it to rebuild her nest for a second brood. The nest was cosily tucked in among the honeysuckle that rambles up the drainpipes in a cold north-west corner and winds its way up on to the flat roof below our bathroom window. A little later that evening I heard the sweetest song; Mr. Blackbird was perched on the windowsill singing an evening hymn of happiness to his best beloved who was fluffed out and cuddled low on her nest.

Spotted flycatchers are everywhere; they are also called Post Birds since they sit on top of any post near human habitation and sing so sweetly. Pied flycatchers have occasionally been seen too, at Huntfield.

Monday 19th The heat is still with us, quite unseasonably. The burns running off the hills are almost dry and already we are trying not to use too much water. The greenhouses are much cooler with "summer cloud" brushed on to the glass, but so far the ones at Dalemain are unpainted so that the fruit trees get as much sun as possible, though the pot plants really need more shade. Polythene which had been tacked under the glass before Christmas is still *in situ* helping to keep a moist atmosphere. During the winter it conserved the heat, keeping the temperature about 5° higher than normal.

Tuesday 20th *Dalemain.*   Woke at 5 a.m. to the sound of rain pattering on the leaves and the swish of water on the road as a car passed through the park; that glorious noise of water and the cool smell of dampness, and low clouds which meant rain. I could have sung for joy on looking out of my window across the lawn; it really was raining, and must have been for some time as the ground was quite wet under the trees. Rose at 5.30 a.m. to see that the flowers in the house looked good, and to rearrange some of the vases, since we were motoring to London to see the Chelsea Flower Show. Gathered half open beech leaves in Lobb's Wood where the early morning sunlight fretted and danced through the undergrowth; it was like Heaven, and though it takes a long time to make the many flower arrangements needed for so large a house, it gives immense pleasure and relaxation so long as one is not in a hurry. The beech leaves looked beautiful in the Chinese drawing room, and on the deep white-washed window-sill half-way down the scrubbed oak stairs – these were built to be Sir Edward's "new front stairs" in the old part of the house, about 1680. With late narcissi and a few tulips, the leaves take on a fretted and elegant appearance against the background of the tall laticed window.

The rain made everything smell quite delicious. When Brian arrived at 8 a.m. we agreed that we should sing "Now thank we all our God" and "Rejoice! Rejoice! Begone dull care!" because the plants could now revive and grow after a drought of at least six weeks.

Wednesday 21st The Flower Show was full of lovely things as usual, though I missed the stand of Blackmore and Langdon's delphiniums in the centre of the marquee through which one used to wander among the magnificent spikes of one of my favourite flowers. It must be more and more expensive to stage these stands. One of the most charming stands was of dwarf bearded irises from V. H. Humphrey of Nottingham. There were so many forms and varieties. Some will certainly be ordered since most varieties of iris flower profusely at Dalemain. One of the taller blue varieties, Derwentwater, bought a few years ago at the Highland Show has been in bloom for some weeks and makes a wonderful show. Bearded Iris like to grow near or on the surface of the soil or

May   even in gravel in order to be baked by the sunshine; Huntfield is usually too cool and damp for these iris to flower well, though they grow and multiply instead.

Thursday 22nd   One of the most beautiful stands was Notcutts. An arched bridge spanned their stand and hundreds of admiring people must have gazed down upon the wealth of flowering cherry trees, deutias, philadelphus and other blossom.

Friday 23rd   We arrived home full of ideas and aspirations, my hold-all full of lists and catalogues so that plants can be ordered peacefully when one has time to consider where new treasures should be planted.

Saturday 24th   We were back at Dalemain in time for a busy Whit holiday weekend, having visited three other houses open to the public en route. It is most interesting to see other historic houses and to gain ideas for our own, but best of all to look at beautiful furniture and pictures. Some of the smallest pieces of furniture are made of fascinating woods such as tulip and laburnum, and one wonders if these were sometimes made by a local craftsman out of a favourite garden tree. We had a very good lunch in a fine orangery where a little boy and his friends were having a birthday party. Not one of these houses had bowls of flowers to grace their stately rooms; a few potted plants were in evidence, very well grown, but they sadly lacked the beauty and the scents of the little posy bowls of polyanthus and primroses from the woods, the sprays of cherry blossom, and the many varieties of narcissi which the visitors admire so much at Dalemain at this time of year.

Sunday 25th   Apart from a little rain last Tuesday, there had been none since. The frames needed much more watering and the greenhouses would have baked at the weekend if we had not arrived home.

Monday 26th   Managed to pot up a lot of nice bushy geranium cuttings of all sorts and put these and a variety of other plants on the stall. It was safe to stand the large old pots of arum lilies round the pool; they were full of flowers, and caused much interest. Fortunately there were a number of young plants showing flower and these too were put out for sale and quickly disappeaared. We had a busy weekend, but it would be very dull for us all, and particularly for the house guides who take so much trouble to understand the history of the house and our family, if there were not plenty of visitors to listen to them.

Tuesday 27th   The Blue Poppies, the lovely Himalayan *Meconopsis grandis*, were coming into bloom. So many people have never heard of a *blue* poppy and there they were growing well in little groups all over the garden, their stately deep blue flowers nodding graciously above their furry pointed leaves which often look somewhat

May   reddy-brown on their undersides. So many gardening visitors asked for plants, and to save time, I dug some of the young plants out of the selling border near the frames with a large lump of soil, and put them into cartons with strawy manure to keep them damp. In an hour they were all sold. It is so difficult to have the right plants at the right moment when one has to do so much oneself. If one can produce more unusual plants, different from the average nursery garden, one can try to build up a reputation. Plants such as the *Meconopsis*, grown in small quantities in a private garden grow to a much bigger size than one can normally buy from a commercial enterprise.

Wednesday 28th   *Huntfield.*   We motored on over the Beef Tub and down the Tweed. It was like a different world, so green and quiet. No traffic up there and the river was fuller than it had been the previous week when we passed on our way to Dalemain; it was as if we were having the glories of spring all over again. Huge old elm trees in the valley were covered with blossom the colour of primroses, and thankfully, no sign of the dreaded disease; oyster catchers were busy fishing undisturbed from rocky pedestals. Small groups of black-faced ewes and lambs were grazing contentedly in sheltered places on the hillside where the short sweet unfertilized grasses were becoming daily greener.

Thursday 29th   At home spotted flycatchers were sitting in wobbly fashion on the beech branches, their beaks always holding firmly on to a worm or fly for their fledgelings who were constantly anxiously waiting for yet another meal. There was a flycatcher in the greenhouse fluttering about in the white jessamine that ramps along the wall behind the staging; they are regular and welcome visitors searching for flies and pests. Cherry blossom everywhere and primulas of all sorts flowering like happy children at the seaside, particularly *Primula Sieboldii*. This variety is the newest one to be sown for these gardens, and as their crinkly leaves emerged from the soil, they became quite exciting to watch since they are very different to the other primulas in the garden; they look quite Chinese when their clear coloured flowers bloom, almost as if they had been painted on eighteenth century porcelain. They had been sown two years past and were truly at their height of beauty, growing in the shady side of the garden near the honeysuckle pergola. Must remember to sow another variety of primula before the growing season is over; this happens all too quickly; seeds sown later in the summer never seem to germinate so well, and it is fun to try something new each year.

Friday 30th   Azaleas were scenting the air, particularly the old yellow ponticum with its grey-green sticky sepals at the back of every flower-head. In spite of the newer and more flamboyant varieties there are none equal to this old fashioned friend.
       Beside the largest of the sweet-smelling azaleas, the glorious flame-coloured maple *Atropurpureum dissectum* grows in the Wild Garden close to the house

May opposite the kitchen door. It seemed to have spread its branches even further in every direction than when I last saw it. When we first came to live at Huntfield over twenty years ago, the yellow azalea was half-buried under vast laurel bushes, now cut back to form an effective windbreak.

There was so much to see and so much to do, and not nearly enough time to see to everything. Hundreds of seedlings needed pricking out or planting out whenever there was a free moment; there were not nearly enough hours in the day, but on the other hand, how frustrating life must be if one has nothing to do.

June
Sunday 1st The seedling Norway maples growing close to the drive side were in yellow leaf catching the arrows of the slanting sunbeams. The avenue, from the road up to the house, had once more taken on its cathedral-like form, as we drove up through a tunnel of beeches, maples, and horse chestnuts, while the dark yews, the ancient silver firs, and the graceful Hemlock Spruce form a wonderful background for their deciduous brethren. Carpets of greenery everywhere concealing hiding places for myriads of birds – gold-crested wrens live in this wood and occasionally brown squirrels. What a paradise after the noise and rush of London.

Monday 2nd After a reasonably warm day with some heavy showers, the evening cleared out for frost; so at 10.30 p.m. I covered the frames, particularly the ones planted with early potatoes which were well up; another frame was planted with bush marrows. Having just cleaned out the greenhouses putting fuschias and arum lilies out in the rain, they were hurriedly put back inside for the night. As I walked back to the house, the huge bushes of yellow azalea were smelling so sweetly even at this late hour; they shone like gold as if the sun was still high in the heavens, but it was the moon, full and brilliant in the near mid-summer sky, that was playing false illusions.

Tuesday 3rd Being so high up, the frost damage passed us, following the course of the burn which runs above the garden. The outdoor potatoes were unscathed as were the tender leaves of *Rodgersia sambucifolia* which frequently succumb at this time of year; but a few miles away at a lower level the potatoes in Skirling village were blackened. As the moon went to bed, the early morning sky away to the north was rosy red, as in some impressionist painting. Is this to be yet another sailor's warning?

Wednesday 4th *Dalemain.* Back at Dalemain where the weather was hot and sultry. Started to bed out the *Begonia semperflorens* in the four beds round the pool in the Knott Garden which had lately been filled with forget-me-nots and wallflowers. Joe was clipping the little boxwood hedges as he has done for years, and we dug in plenty of good rotted manure topped with leaf-mould. The hedges and the spring bedding take a lot out of the ground and begonias need a damp soil

June   rich in humus. The boxes of begonias which were pricked out at Huntfield had developed much better than the ones left at Dalemain. It must have been the cooler conditions and the richer peaty soil which brought them on so well.

Thursday 5th   Last year at the Highland Show we bought a little trailer to go behind the car, which has since proved invaluable. On this last journey it was filled with bedding plants, and blue poppies potted up in plastic pots for the stall, shrub roses, likewise potted up, and other little treasures.

     Thunder rumbled round all day, and it was certain that the brewing storm would break. The air was full of electricity, and that eerie feeling of the incomprehensible. I was busy digging up various herbaceous plants for such a nice lady visitor from Middlesborough when I realised that we should hurry, and only just reached the potting shed as the storm broke above us. How much we needed the rain, but not quite the torrent in which it fell at that moment. The plants were boxed up, and as I carried them across to the house, one of the horse-chestnut trees on "the green" felt as if it had been struck by lightning right above me. The noise was frightening, but it was not the tree that had been struck, but the electric pylon up in the Deer Park. The plants were piled into the car for their new owner while the courtyard became a small lake.

Saturday 7th   It was almost exciting after the storm subsided. Our little world felt so fresh and cool; the birds sang more clearly and the garden was refreshed. Everything seemed to have grown in stature overnight.

Sunday 8th   Planted out fuschias in the Knott Garden with little carpets of String of Pearl and Cambridge Blue Lobelia beneath them. The dahlias, planted a few days ago, were standing up straight and the arum lilies round the pool looked beautiful. Since there is not enough heat to bring these on in readiness for Easter, they can become a feature at this time of year. It is extraordinary how they harbour greenfly in company with fuschias, and a smoke bomb is necessary to be put into operation in order to kill the greenfly before moving the plants from the greenhouse.

Monday 9th   *Huntfield.*   Back at Huntfield to a world of azaleas and blue poppies. The Dacre W.I. will be here next week for their summer outing and I hope the garden will look as beautiful then, as it is at present. The avenue of laburnums are heavy with blossom. These were planted about twenty years ago and look wonderful as one walks beneath their cascades of golden flowers. Most of them were self-sown seedlings from the tree at the corner of the terrace at Dalemain.

     The thunder storm had caused one laburnum to fall right over beneath its weight of blossom. They are such shallow rooted trees, but it may be possible to prop it up again with some fencing stobs, straining wire, and a piece of an old gum boot to prevent the tree from rubbing aginst the wire.

     There is so much weeding to do, interspersed with desperately-needed

June planting out. Lovely plants of *Monarda*, the sweet-scented bergamot used by the monks and herbalists long ago, were transferred with plenty of earth, from frames to borders. Likewise, *Coreopsis* Mayfield Giant almost too tall to move, but with a good watering these well-rooted plants grown from cuttings may never realize they have been moved.

Wednesday 11th Fuschias seem to be rabbit-proof, so a couple of nice young plants of the pale pink hardy fuschia were planted in the paeony border near the drawing room door. This border used to be a mass of roses, partially netted, until the rabbits became intolerable and the roe deer took their young for midnight strolls, nipping off the roses as they passed. The roses suffered so badly and never recovered, so paeonies are bravely taking over, with Japanese irises interspersed with rodgersias and an edging of golden thyme. It remains to be seen if these are left untouched.

Thursday 12th When I was a child, begonias were planted profusely by my grandfather at Lanrick Castle, a large and very comfortable nineteenth-century moated house beside the glorious river Teith in Perthshire. The castle had been built around a much earlier fortified tower, the word Lanrick meaning "A clearing in the forest". So it still seemed to me as a small child where huge Wellingtonias, Douglas Firs, Hemlock Spruce, and many more grew to immense height and girth in the soft clime of the area. The walled gardens were a long way from the house; one walked along neatly-raked paths above the river to reach them; seedling trees covered the mossy fern-haunted banks. Verdant lawns stretched down to the river from the castle, and on either side of the gravel path near the moat were at least a dozen round beds filled with begonias, edged with a thick frill of white alyssum, each bed a perfect carpet of flowers. There were plenty of rabbits in those days, enough to pay Jimmy Ure, the keeper's wage, but none of these beds were protected with rabbit netting.

With this in mind I planted a box of *Begonia semperflorens* in the border near the house, with fuschias behind to give height. The two urns on either side of the kitchen door were filled with "Caledonia", a soft pink geranium that always produces a large head. Silver-leaved ballotta flowed over the edges with blue lobelia, safely out of the reach of Benjamin Bunny.

Friday 13th *Dalemain.* Coltsfoot very bad among the strawberries. Meant to use Tumbleweed or its less expensive agricultural counterpart, Roundup, but a little dangerous when the fruit is colouring. So the coltsfoot was forked and pulled out instead, but must be killed by some deep running weedkiller later on. The kitchen garden at Dalemain was neglected for years, but disliking weedkillers and their effects on the earth and its worms and insect population, we have persevered with hand weeding. Jerusalem artichokes look well and provide a useful winter vegetable, besides being a beneficial ground cleaner. They are

June   difficult to peel economically by hand, but a good clean in the electric potato peeler is sufficient, and when served with a white sauce and chopped parsley, they are a delicious vegetable. We manage to have fresh or dried parsley from the garden all the year round.

Sunday 15th   Very heavy thundery rain; thunder storms crashing somewhere over Haweswater. Managed to plant up dwarf sweet williams in the half-moon bed beside the Grove, on the front of the house, where aconites had formed a thick carpet in the early months. When these were dead and dry, we covered the bed with leaf-mould and some manure; into this mixture the sweet williams were carefully lifted, since most were already flowering. Behind these the alchemillas, the dear Lady's Mantle, was already in bloom. These seed so freely that it seems really best to remove the old plants each back-end so that they do not overpower the aconites. Their fresh pale yellow flowers make the most lovely foil for sweet peas or roses in floral arrangements, softly falling over the edge of perhaps a bowl of flowers on a small table in the drawing room. Their usefulness and beauty is unlimited.

Monday 16th   *Huntfield.*   A lovely day spent at the Highland Show. Kelways had a fine stand of paeonies as usual, but one missed many of the old friends such as Jack Drake who introduced the magnificent *Meconopsis grandis*. Bought a nice white fuschia which had already broken a strong branch. What cuttings that were possible from this branch, were inserted in a sandy mixture when we arrived home.

Tuesday 17th   The Dacre W.I. members arrived in a bus at Huntfield for their summer outing. Having talked to them about this garden at one of their winter meetings, they decided to come and see it for themselves. There were many old friends among the party whom I had known all my life, and who were interested to come and visit our Scottish garden. They were fascinated by the blue poppies and the many varieties of candelabra primulas. After a good tea at which our dearest grand-children, David, now eighteen months, and Saya who is only six months, made an appearance, the Dacre ladies went on their way, pronouncing this to have been their best outing yet!

The Blue Poppies, *Meconopsis grandis*, make the most wonderful display at this time of year, and for many weeks, and grow so easily in this soil, multiplying as prolifically as herbaceous plants. There are big groups on the edge of the lawn, their large deep blue saucer-like faces shining resplendently against the background of dark conifers or rhododendrons. Further up, above the house, groups of the older variety *Baileyi* also look well with paler blue and somewhat smaller flowers. It was surprising how well *Meconopsis* became established at Dalemain in a completely different soil; the richer the soil the better the colour. During the last years sackloads of these magnificent plants have travelled from their Scottish home to their new abode in Cumbria, where

The Elizabethan gazebo, built on a strategic point at the top of the High Garden, with phloxes in the foreground.

Looking North at Huntfield in May where azaleas and rhododendrons and meconopsis grow with a ground cover of spring flowers.

The magnificent well-head in the Rose Garden at Huntfield. Roseraie de L'Hay, a hardy shrub rose that smells of sugared almonds, is underbedded with a profusion of Lady's Mantle.

they too have repaid all my care; they have been a constant source of delight since purchasing the first three plants many years ago, and from which all these have grown.

Dalemain. Continued bedding out whenever possible. Everyone speaks of the slowness of growth after May's early drought. The marrows have scarcely moved since they were planted out in empty frames to which a generous amount of good rotted manure was incorporated with the soil.

Filled up the permanently planted beds in the Knott Garden wherever there were spaces. Two of these beds are filled with golden marjoram among which *Allium ostrowskianum* planted last autumn are just showing colour. Two other beds are filled with violas on the shadier side of the garden. I like the whole-coloured viola faces better than pansies for this garden; they have already produced a lot of colour and were now filled up with old-fashioned lilac blue viola, Maggi Mott. Two other beds are already full of dwarf lavender, Munstead, which needs to be clipped regularly, and two more with pinks. It is difficult to put farm manure among these closely-knit perennials; instead barrowloads of well-rotted leaf-mould were scattered among the plants, which will certainly help the pinks and violas to layer themselves and thereby rejuvenate the old plants. A little dried blood was also scattered except among the marjoram which grows very freely.

Planted the two round central beds at each end of the Knott Garden with half-hardy semi-standard fuschias, cotton lavender, double bedding dahlias and nemesia. Celandines are a problem but we dug out what was possible, and after cleaning and planting the celandines had disappeared for another year. They are such beautiful flowers and really should be encouraged to grow for their own sake. At Huntfield they grow profusely in the damp gravel near the house and make a cheerful border in springtime.

Midsummer, but not the weather we expect in June; driving rain and blustery winds. As usual the "Delphinium Wind" has come upon us; it invariably attempts to knock down these glorious plants just as they are coming into flower. The wire hoops made from all the "left-overs" from fencing had been installed in time this year, giving tremendous protection and making early staking very simple. Picked a few half-opened blooms for the vase on the window-sill half-way up the White stairs. Here, facing north west, it is cool and flowers last quite a long time.

Sprays of the tiny Threepennybit rose Farreri were also gathered for the bowl on the elegant three-cornered basin stand in the drawing room, and lilac, still blooming profusely, scented the Chinese drawing room. This lilac was a very strong-growing American hybrid, called Elinor, which must be thirty feet high and liberally covered with claret pink blooms. Its paler

June   counterpart, Bellicent, had just finished blooming. Both varieties are very easy to root as cuttings.

Wednesday 25th   Tremendous thunderstorms constantly coming so suddenly and as they approach the birds become very quiet until the storm is past. Half a mile up the estate road in the meadow near Dacre Castle there was not a drop of rain, and silage making continued without interruption.

I spent these thundery interludes repotting a mass of greenhouse plants badly in need of a shift. Geraniums of many varieties, fuschias and pelargoniums, and all the cuttings taken this spring needed potting or repotting; agapanthus too, were split up and put into eight and nine inch pots for the stall with rotted manure in the mixture to feed the plants and to provide the moisture they need.

Thursday 26th   As I came out of the greenhouse a whole charm of goldfinches flew out of the barrow left outside on the gravel. They must have been eating seeds from forget-me-nots and groundsel lying in the barrow, and like little flashes of gold, they darted in all directions above the stately blue delphinium border and over the dark yew hedge in search of more seed.

Friday 27th   Shrub roses are covering themselves with flowers of a hundred hues. The earliest varieties are fading, passing away all too quickly for yet another season. About twenty-five years ago, two enormous beech trees standing at the top of a little stone stairway at the end of the terrace blew in a gale and came down on part of the vinery which was never replaced. After the debris had been cleared and the other half of the vinery made good, the ground was planted with a few shrubs and shrub roses, some of which outgrew their allotted space and were removed; one of the remaining roses is *Hugonis*, an enormous shrub which is always smothered in primrose-coloured flowers and the most beautiful fern-like foliage some of which turns gold and amber in the autumn. It is always the first rose to bloom, and the visitors stand and stare at the profusion of its blossom and are frequently amazed to be told it is a rose. Like Robert Herrick who mourned the passing of the fair daffodils, I too mourn the passing of these pale beauties, their semi-single faces upturned towards the early summer sunshine.

The scarlet-thorned species *Rosa pyracantha* also blooms early with small snow-white single flowers taking second place to the handsome but dangerous thorns.

Saturday 28th   In their place the pink and deep reds and purple roses are blooming, the Empress Josephine, luscious and scented, and Constance Spry, voluptuous and prolific, each bloom like a loose-petalled paeony; many more shrub roses each one different in form and hue bloom in the long border that wanders up the hill to the summer-house where, if there is time to sit and stare, and think,

June one can look down upon the whole of the walled garden, a theme in many variations; up on the old brick Tudor walls at the further end, morello cherries ramble, and beyond and above these walls the varied roofs and chimney stacks of home sit comfortably together, silhouetted against the ever-changing sky.

Sunday 29th On the front of the house the Old China rose is wreathed in glory. These bushes have been growing for at least a hundred years and where some of them died in the bad winter of 1968, the tall-growing floribunda Anna Louise was planted as replacement. These reach the high window-sills with ease as do the China rose, but two later replacements of Anna Louise must have been grown on dwarf stocks and look out of keeping; they should be replaced if possible in the autumn. The old Blush China Rose, also called the Monthly Rose from its incessant blooming, was introduced in 1718 and is well worth growing. It is one of the most important ancestors of our modern perpetual-flowering roses.

Monday 30th Poured all day. It was a lovely early morning and I collected flowers for the house. As I came indoors it began to rain; these clusters of clouds bring hours of rain – such a beautiful expression "a cluster of clouds" which is what the weatherman foretold.

It was a day for the potting shed and pricking out the endless seedlings all waiting for a shift. Always keeping a potting mixture ready makes such days much easier. Added another barrowload of lovely rotted beech leaf-mould to the mixture and with a sack of moss off the hill for the base of every box and pot, it was plain sailing. Rock roses came first, followed by dianthus, *Allwoodii alpinus* – about one hundred seedlings, now mostly nice little plants all from one packet of seed; then polyanthus – about eighty smaller seedlings went into wooden boxes, while the larger ones were boxed up roughly to keep them fresh till I can prick them out into a frame where they stay until the spring, again all from one packet of seed. If one leaves them rather longer than one should in the seed pan, smaller seedlings develop and it is these which usually produce the best and most unusual colours. The seeds must be sown very thinly so that they do not ruin one another.

July
Wednesday 2nd Lilies planted in nine-inch pots are looking well, until recently buried up to the rims in one of the leaf-mould clamps. These bulbs have been grown for two or three years in pots; each autumn they are buried and covered in the leaf-mould clamp where they remain until they are in bud. When new shoots begin to emerge, the leaf-mould is pushed back, the frost being well past. Occasionally they are given a feed of Sangral. They do not all survive and I wish I could manage to keep the more recherché varieties for longer. Auratums and regales are fairly reliable, but do not survive more than two or three years, while the hardier lilies such as Enchantment and Harmony survive for many seasons. Potted lilies like to stand cool and airy on the east side of the

July   garden wall. Black Dragon, Green Dragon, and Longiflorum and the like are so lovely, but all so expensive to replace nowadays. A few pots of lilies in flower look and smell exotic standing in the house, some of the American hybrids such as Enchantment with its glowing orange flowers multiply in the garden forming sizable clumps if one can find the right place to suit their needs. Mice and voles take their toll, and although the soil conditions in part of the Low Garden are good for lilies, the odd rabbit manages to find its way to nip off the growing shoots at the worst possible moment; lily shoots must be particularly succulent. Leaf-mould or peat is very beneficial to scatter around clumps of lilies particularly the stem-rooting varieties.

Thursday 3rd   The paeonies are really good this year with a profusion of large flower heads in many shades of pink and white and some like large saucers with beautiful yellow stamens. During the spring self-sown forget-me-nots had run riot among them making a wonderful show of gentian blue beneath an overhanging damson tree whose white blossom shone like driven snow against the dark bark of the branches. We managed to uproot most of the forget-me-nots just before they seeded everywhere and forked a truckload of manure among the paeonies while the ground below was still damp. This mulch has helped greatly to keep the weed population in check.

Friday 4th   Arranged a large jug on the hall table with paeonies and Lady's Mantle, that soft and elegant yellow-green plant which graces any vase of flowers.

Brian and I cleaned the "Children's" gardens near the summer-house. These are now mainly filled with old striped roses under which blue geraniums act as ground cover. Jessamine rambles up the wall at the back while snowdrops and aconites peep out from the shelter of its straggly growth early in the year. When I was a child a little path edged with flagstones traversed each of the Children's gardens and there I made a burial ground for all the unfortunate birds, sadly mourning the loss of every feathered friend.

On the wall against the Elizabethan summer-house the actinidia is beginning to climb, lending colour to a somewhat dull corner. This slender twining climber has spectacular coloured foliage with large heart-shaped leaves turning from green to pink and cream and is well worth planting.

Edna sprinkled caustic soda on the pink sandstone steps leading down into this summer-house, and after a good swill with clean water the following day they looked clean and a beautiful colour after being covered with mosses for a very long time. She cleaned the steps leading down into Lobbs Wood and those that led from the terrace into the Low Garden in the same way; they have never been cleaned properly for many years, and at last they looked important and attractive.

This summer-house is fascinating with its pointed roof and ancient timbers radiating from a king post in the apex; mullioned windows overlook the beck where kingfishers live undisturbed.

July *Sunday 6th*	The long herbaceous border on the terrace is simply wreathed in Sticky Willie, and I started a battle to eradicate this persistent plant called by many different names – cleavers, goose-grass, or Jack-run-about-the-hedge. It was only just beginning to come into flower, so if it can only be pulled out before it sets its tiny green cannon ball seeds, all will be well. The only way to succeed is to delve in among the roots of the plants in the border and pull the sticky gentleman out at its base, when it can then be pulled away from the tops of herbaceous plants which it covers in unwanted garlands.
Monday 7th	Continued to clean the border. The thick mulch of farm manure has paid off dividends – there were scarcely any other weeds. Three years ago when dear Uncle Godfrey tried to help me, the weeds of all sorts were terrible. Uncle Godfrey, then in his eighty-eighth year, was a madly keen gardener and a lover of all country matters. He had spent much of his childhood at Dalemain which he loved dearly, and latterly always gave me money for birthdays and Christmas to buy trees or shrubs for the garden. The *Magnolia stellata* now growing into quite a bush was one of these presents and walnut trees near the old hound kennels were another. It is a cosy feeling to see these trees growing when such a dear person is lying peacefully in Dacre churchyard. We were always anxious in case he should fall, or slip in his heavy wellington boots, but he persisted in weeding and pruning. One day as he cut the ivy back from the Low Garden wall, he slipped on the stone steps and cut his head, but in spite of this nasty episode he gardened whenever he could. A very heavy shower fell at tea-time, spoiling fields of hay lying cut or turned which needed only a few sunny days for all to be made safe. About half past eight in the evening the mists rose along the meadow like a great white blanket. We watched fascinated, for usually an evening mist of this nature means a hot day to follow.
Tuesday 8th	Morning dawned, glorious and hot, but though it clouded over, the day stayed dry. A Flower Club from Consett came to visit Dalemain and to buy many unusual plants from the garden. The flowers in the house looked really lovely – philadelphus, delphiniums, shrub roses, paeonies, and a few of the first sweet peas. The vase on the window-sill on the white stairs was mostly of delphiniums and lady's mantle, and this, standing out against the white-washed walls, was the one which the Flower Club members admired most.
Wednesday 9th	Raspberries are ripening fast, and are a very good crop, due probably to being well mulched, which also helps to keep the weeds down. Strawberries are only a fair crop since they badly lacked rain in May and June. Birds everywhere despite netting, and it is a race as to which of us will get the most fruit. A wren has built a charming nest in the lowest branch of the Grecian Silver Fir at the end of the terrace. As it is so low above the gravel walk where visitors meander,

July   I do pray that Mrs. Wren will not desert it, or her young ones who regularly
peep out of their dome-shaped home. Watched the pied wagtail pop into a
hole in the Deer Park wall to feed her young, while a yellow wagtail is feeding
a second brood in the jessamine beside the kitchen window in the courtyard.
Goldfinches flitting about among the weeds in the kitchen garden, and the
swallows which had been reared in the roof of the potting shed above the
bench, flew last evening. Swallows always seem to bring luck.

Friday 11th   *Huntfield.*   Potted up three dozen *Erinus alpinus* for the stall. The garden walls
at Huntfield are now covered with this beautiful rock plant having spread
from a few seedlings planted a few years ago. The Romans are said to have
brought the erinus to Britain and it is to be found on some of their forts on
Hadrian's Wall.
    There was not sufficient time to pot up all the seedlings before returning to
Huntfield by train on this occasion, so I took the wooden seed box back with
me inside a laundry box for safety. The good work can be continued, so that
the remainder of the newly potted erinus can make the return journey next
week. I wonder how many other people have done such mad things as to
travel on a train with such an extraordinary parcel. When Bryce met me at
Carstairs Station he thought I was more eccentric than usual!

Sunday 13th   Spotted flycatchers are fascinating to watch at Huntfield. Another brood has
recently hatched, and they flit about among the cotoneaster hedge and perch
on top of posts which hold rabbit netting up in the Wild Garden close to the
kitchen window.
    It almost feels as if one is living in the midst of a woodland garden one is so
close to the birds.

Monday 14th   Planted out three hundred leeks in a nice cool place behind the rose pergola
where Davy had dug in plenty of manure. That dreadful weed Betony, known
as Fat-Hen in the north, is one of the real plagues to the Huntfield garden. It
has brittle lengthy white roots that go to enormous depths wherever one is
unfortunate enough to drop a piece when weeding. The more one digs and
cleans the worse it seems to grow. Betony and convolvulus were both here
when we arrived, and though we have dug and cleaned continuously, it is
always with us. Next spring we must try one of the selective weedkillers
whenever they appear above soil level.

Tuesday 15th   Pricked out a mass of coloured cowslip seedlings in the same border. It was
very hot, so kneeling on a sack in the shade was very pleasant. It is so essential
to prick out seedlings in good time to give them both space and food to grow
on. Frequently one has no time, or perhaps groundsel needs hoeing in another
part of the garden and seedlings suffer as a result.

July	*Dalemain.* An article I had written called "Living Between Two Gardens"
Wednesday 16th	appeared in the *Cumberland and Westmorland Herald* at the weekend and several

July
Wednesday 16th

Dalemain. An article I had written called "Living Between Two Gardens" appeared in the *Cumberland and Westmorland Herald* at the weekend and several people told me how much they had enjoyed it. I wrote about the joys of having two springs and two of so many things because the winter lasts so much longer at Huntfield; but this brings compensations, for one has a prolonged season of daffodils, primroses and most other flowers. One can grow a wider variety of plants in the different soils and though one struggles to make the most loved plants grow equally well in both gardens it is not always possible. There are different birds too; the wild geese seldom fly or rest upon the land at Dalemain, and equally it is only in that gentler clime that kingfishers flash their colours. I often wish there was more time to write of the wonders of nature.

Saturday 19th

Huntfield. A large rabbit bolted across the lawn by the pool inside the walled garden. However carefully we shut gates they still dig their way occasionally under the old walls. I thought one had managed to find a way in since pansies and *campanula persicifolia* are being eaten continuously. Huntfield has been alive with rabbits since the spring. The previous long hard winter drove them to gnaw and kill the lovely hornbeam hedge dividing the lawns from the field which we planted at least fifteen years ago. The beech hedges were stripped of their bark and likewise bled to death when the sap began to rise. Many good shrubs were overtaken by the same fate, including a handsome parrotia whose flame-coloured leaves glowed against the dark green of an old Wellingtonia in the Wild Garden. One ceases to have any enthusiasm for planting outside the walled garden.

Sunday 20th

Two red squirrels crossed our path as we returned from church. Once there were many squirrels around, but not now. Since our family crest is a squirrel proper, with bushy tail, eating a hazel nut, we always feel that when one crosses our path luck will cross it also. It takes five acres of conifer, preferably pine, to support a pair of squirrels.

Monday 21st

On returning to Huntfield the most welcome parcel of seeds had arrived from Thomson & Morgan including a packet of *Salvia turkestanica* which I feared was unobtainable. I could have danced for joy since my precious boxful of plants, which were more than ready to line out, had been stolen at Dalemain – a whole wooden apple box had simply disappeared. We seldom lose anything in the garden that has been noticeable, though one Sunday when neither Brian nor I were around every single rose off the watering cans was taken from the greenhouse. A friend had generously given me half her packet of *Turkestanica* since she had only a small garden and these seedlings had been carefully tended since they were sown the previous autumn; they should have been planted out a month ago, but as usual, there was not enough time and so they sat in the wooden box in a sheltered shady place at the end of the cold frames until somebody else realized their worth.

July
Tuesday 22nd

With a good mixture to hand, I filled a number of propagating seed pans, covering them with plastic lids. They were put into a shaded part of the greenhouse with a cover of black polythene until germination takes place.

Also sowed *Salvi superba*, *Linium flavum*, *Linium nurbonense*, *Clematis tangutica*, *Saponaria*, *Lychnis chalcedonica* and rock campanulas.

Wednesday 23rd

The old plants of *Clematis tangutica* had been killed in the long cold winter of 1978-79 which were a sad loss, rambling over archways in the garden where their yellow Chinese lampshade-like flowers bloomed in profusion for many seasons; these were followed by silver-green fluffy seedheads which lasted all winter, looking extremely ornamental. Other seedlings sown about a month or more ago had mainly germinated well; they are safe in a shaded frame without a glass. Delphiniums and polyanthus looked very promising.

The milkman horrified us when he said that the ground was quite frosty last week in the early mornings. Terrible to have frost possibly in every single month of the year in this area.

Thursday 24th

Potted up various plants for the stall; plants which will soon be in flower, and for which visitors will ask when they see them blooming in the garden. Unless the would-be buyers are gardeners in the true sense, they seldom buy plants which are not in flower. *Phygelius capensis*, the Cape Figwort, makes a great show with flame-coloured tubular flowers, growing easily close to a south or west wall, was potted up besides many varieties of candelabra primulas – the flame Inverewe hybrid and others, pink, clarets, and yellows; they all grow so easily at Huntfield seeding about in the cool and always damp soil, but it is more difficult to get them to grow well at Dalemain where the ground bakes and cracks.

Davy and I started to clean the Wild Garden which was becoming quite a jungle. The Black Iris, *chrysographes*, were growing profusely mixed up with the roots of a poor michaelmas daisy, so I lifted hefty clumps and dug the ground, which is shaded by a huge old-fashioned moschata floribunda rose, and a purple-leaved berberis. The irises divided into dozens of plants, enough to take plenty to Dalemain and to make a good bed as well. Near these the red primulas, Millars Crimson, were even seeding into the grass. It is a very damp, badly drained area of the garden, and suits the primula family admirably. Lifted the largest of these seedlings to plant elsewhere.

In another "bed" in the Wild Garden the latest acquisition from Jack Drake's nursery a year ago were three Primulas called Red Sunset and almost past flowering. Cleaned this piece of ground and replanted the primulas which divided into about fifteen good plants. What a wonderful return for three small plants – hopefully they may seed safely on the clean ground. The waterlily colchicums have produced clusters of corms and should make a good show in October if the weather is kind: they are a very ornamental variety.

July
Tuesday 29th

Dalemain. The roses at Dalemain are simply wonderful with huge flower-heads. They have certainly benefited from the mulch given late in the spring. It is so hot and thundery one can scarcely work, but I hoed and cleaned the big bed of roses where groundsel would soon be seeding.

Delphiniums are enormous this year; again mulching carefully has helped. They become too tall and difficult to stake, and the constant hot muggy weather and many thundery storms have toppled some of the tallest although the wire netting guards have done much to keep them upright. It is important to put Slug Death around these plants whose juicy young growths are a very tasty bite.

Moved the big pots of agapanthus round the pool in place of arum lilies which must now rest. Old Stuart always laid arums on their sides behind the garden wall and brought them indoors in early September when they start to grow for another season's bloom. All plants must rest at some season or they become exhausted.

Thursday 31st

Some of the seedlings sown ten days ago have already germinated – the first which really cheered my spirit were two trays of *Salvia turkestanica*. I felt so thrilled to see them safely through. Two years ago when I had really good plants in full flower, the visitors thought they were wonderful, few having any idea what they were. One group of people remarked that there was nothing like them even in the famous gardens at Harlow Car, which was quite a compliment. Lilac-pink flowers always seem to appeal to visitors. In drier areas *Salvia turkestanica* seeds itself and the seedlings survive the winter, but being a woolly-leafed plant, the dampness of the Lake District is death to many plants of this type, and one needs to sow them by hand.

August
Friday 1st

Huntfield. It was very hot weather and at last the hay is being safely gathered in. Flies are very troublesome and wasps are prolific this year at Huntfield. The strawberry bed seems to be quite unsafe to enter as there are wasp bikes in the redcurrants on the wall behind.

The huge old-fashioned rambling rose, *Floribunda moschata*, which is very similar to the famous Kiftsgate rose, is a mass of bloom. Years ago an old Oxford friend of my father's, Professor Cecil Morrison, was staying at Dalemain and was amazed that we did not grow this rose. He lived somewhere in Dorset; duly cuttings arrived and grew into enormous thorny thickets, but their wealth of cream flowers with warmer coloured centres were worth all the trouble needed to keep them and their horrible thorns within bounds. Another batch of cuttings were planted against a lonicera hedge where they could ramble up pollarded sweet-smelling poplars planted to keep the winds off the rose garden at Huntfield. Later cuttings of the moschata rose were planted against yew trees growing beside the water garden. This part of the garden is really a deep burn flowing down from the hills past the house and the yard where, over the years, I have planted shrubs and herbaceous plants which will look after themselves. It is an ideal place for this rambling rose and its

page 67

August great sprays of small flowers look beautiful sprawling over and through the dark yews. When the winter comes the oldest wood must be cut out when possible in order to keep the rose within bounds. An enormously tall pale pink spirea grows easily on the bank of the burn while giant-headed valerians, yellow flag irises and a red-barked willow complete the picture; ornamental leaves of *Rodgersia palmatum* turn red and bronze in the sunlight on the top of the bank. They are most rewarding plants to grow, quickly developing into a wealth of foliage which turns and twists in the breeze, changing colour as it does so.

It is quite exciting gazing down from the small stone bridge to watch the water sallying and bubbling below, between the steep banks where this wealth of plant life thrives, and on from dark little pools into the mystery of the woodlands beyond where birds can nest safely and occasionally red squirrels build their dreys.

Tuesday 5th *Dalemain.*   Raspberries, Glenclova, Malling Promise and Malling Jewel have fruited particularly well this year; some of the sixteen-year-old schoolgirls who help to serve refreshments and teas in the Old Hall at Dalemain help to pick the raspberries as well as strawberries and black and red currants in their season. Earlier in the summer we put a good mulch of strawy manure between the lines of rasps, which has both kept the weeds in check and fed the fruit canes. Some of the girls have lately helped to weed in the kitchen garden where groundsel has grown apace in these last weeks of incessantly wet weather. We all struggle on, trying to keep the weeds in check. During these last ten days I have hoed and weeded endlessly in the flower garden which, except for two dirty corners, is now really very clean and full of colour.

Delphiniums are still lovely, but have taken much battering with the wind and rain of late.

Friday 8th The Knott Garden is looking well and a morning was well spent weeding the little boxwood beds. At last the *Begonia semperflorens* are bushing out and covering themselves with bloom. Lavender is a mass of scented heads, and the violas, Lorna and Cornutica have never ceased to flower since early spring; violas and begonias seem to enjoy the wet weather.

A tour of Australian gardeners arrived; they were the most charming party, and were quite enthralled with the garden and the many unusual plants. A large pink herbaceous mallow and its white counterpart caught the eye of Mrs. Jeffrey, a very knowledgeable elderly lady from Victoria who told me much about her own garden. If the weather improves enough for seeds to ripen I hope to be able to send her seed from the mallows they thought so beautiful. Some of their party hope to return another year and stay in our holiday cottages to see the garden once more.

August *Sunday 10th*	Madonna lilies growing in the vine border are truly magnificent. Must order more bulbs before it is too late, for this lilium should be planted very soon, unlike most of the other lilies which prefer spring planting. Lovely yellow trumpet lilies grown in pots are opening. We moved them into a cool part of the greenhouse to shelter them from the heavy rain.

Monday 11th *Huntfield.*   More seeds are through in the seedpans, *Saponaria, Linum narbonense,* and *Clematis tangutica* – the enchanting yellow lampshade clematis. I do hope these will grow on successfully to clothe rustic archways.

Two packets of *Alstroemaria,* the pink-shaded ligtu hybrids which had been sown earlier in four plastic five-inch pots, were making good progress. They had been left in a shady part of the greenhouse with a pane of glass and a sheet of black polythene to cover them, and now looked strong enough to stand outside on the gravel in the warm rainy weather. After two days out of doors they had grown in every way; they will probably winter in a frame or a cold greenhouse where hopefully the small brown mice will not make a meal out of their soft green shoots.

Two enormous old standard fuschias, Swingtime and Eva Borg, shade one end of the greenhouse. I bought them many years ago at the Chelsea Show and planted them in a sheltered border, but sadly one of our usual gales broke their heavy mop-like tops right off. Being sensible plants they soon developed new shoots, and after wintering in pots in the greenhouse it seemed wise to let them remain there; so now, years later and still in ten-inch pots, they have rooted far below and beyond and produce the most magnificent show the entire summer. Each February they are pruned back to two buds more or less all over, though a few branches have been allowed to grow long and are tied on to the beams. Their bells hang from the roof and look beautiful and unusual as one walks under a forest of fuschias. An old fig tree on the back wall puts out shiny green deeply cut leaves to lend a backcloth to the fuschias which are relatively trouble-free. A young "Swingtime" standard is now planted in the greenhouse at Dalemain to grow into something equally beautiful.

Wednesday 13th *Dalemain.*   The Old China rose and the floribunda, Anna Louise, growing on the front of the house at Dalemain are still blooming away. The dressing of Fison's Rose Plus fertilizer a month ago is beginning to tell as the second flowering gets under way. How these roses survive in a very limited root area close to the cellar windows is amazing. They too need mulching, sometimes with grass cuttings from the lawn and sometimes with farm manure, and very important with buckets of water in dry weather. These seven very wet weeks this year have certainly helped them and also the herbaceous plants on the terrace which otherwise droop very quickly in a drought. The original Norman pele tower was built on a rocky bank and in dry weather the border planted on the site of the earlier fortifications suffers as a result.

The Old China rose must have been planted before the turn of the century because it appears in water-colour paintings of that period when my father's older cousins Dorothy and Eva and their Irish mother Maud Flood spent much of their time water-colouring. They were instructed by Edward Hobley, the then art master at Penrith Grammar School, and fortunately these four enthusiastic painters left the only record of so many treasures growing in the garden at that time.

Edward's two daughters Olga and Eva have painted many water-colours in these last summers so that a further record will be left. Today, they brought six more paintings to add to the collection; two are painted from the top of the East Park looking down on to the mediaeval part of the house, the barns and the courtyard, and across the parkland towards Barton Fell. The river Eamont is shown in these pictures where it was dammed in the eighteenth century to form a little lake, so fashionable in those days. I have always admired the soft lights of water-colours, and these paintings may tell future generations the story of the land we have loved so deeply.

Sunday 17th — *Plumbago capensis* in the greenhouse at Dalemain sprawls to the top of the back wall and is becoming covered with flowers of such a heavenly shade of blue. Last autumn it was cut back to about four feet from the ground and about the end of May when it was growing freely I took cuttings of some of the leaders, particularly those growing out over the walk; these rooted easily and are now nice plants growing in three and four inch pots. Early summer seems to be the best time for rooting plumbago; autumn cuttings are difficult to root without proper warm conditions.

Monday 18th — A few seeds were rescued from the tulip tree which has grown on the lawn for a very long time, certainly since before 1860. The birds seem to take most of the seeds when there are any, but what to do with them now so that they will germinate next spring is quite a problem. They should be striated during winter time, but so often mice or other pests eat these precious seeds before they have time to grow. When I was a child, our Nanny always told us that the tulip tree only flowered once in a hundred years and of course *she* had seen it flower; it actually flowers whenever the season is free from frost – lovely yellow waterlily-like flowers high up on the old branches. Continental timber merchants have tried to buy it for furniture making and have been quite indignant on being refused.

Tuesday 19th — *Huntfield.* The tropaeolum at Huntfield is an absolutely wonderful sight. Climbing up through some rather dull rhododendron bushes near the house, it wreaths the dark bushes with flame-coloured flowers for many weeks until frost destroys the blossoms. Many years ago an old lady who lived in a cottage across a field near Gladstone Borelands gave me a few sprouting seedlings carefully dug up in their own earth. The tropaeolum flourished all over her

August overgrown orchard regardless of the overtaking grass. The seedlings were planted beneath the edge of the rhododendrons at the foot of the path leading to the walled garden; there, in the coolness of the leaf-mould and peaty soil, they grew and spread, dropping their black seeds further and further among their hosts.

It is said that tropaeolum does not grow in the south where the summers are too hot. When I was a child it sprawled through and over the high yew hedge at the foot of the Knott Garden, but since then has almost died out because the hedge is cut in mid-May just as the flame flower pushes its way towards the light through the hedge. Seedlings have been successfully moved from Huntfield to Dalemain, but the hedge cutting is a problem weakening the tropaeolum which is a somewhat temperamental plant to move. I must try and establish more seedlings among other shrubs.

Thursday 21st Lately, Archie Elliott, one of our cousins, brought a bag of seedlings from his beautiful garden at Morton House on the edge of Edinburgh. Here it sprawls through a seat and the roses close to his front door. So these were planted in various parts of the garden in order to try and establish this glorious fireball of late summer.

Friday 22nd Heavy rains have battered much of the garden at Huntfield. Groundsel has grown to a great height and everyone is complaining of the weeds in this extraordinary season. Hay crops still lie turned and blackening on most upland farms. What will the fell farmers do to feed their poor flocks this winter?

The pans of seedlings grow well, but are safer covered at least by night in case of heavy rain. The pans of *Salvia turkestanica* are now showing their silvery woolly leaves and cheer me every time I look at them. These seedlings will probably remain where they are until spring when they will be pricked out. Sometimes seedlings pricked out at this time of year are too fragile to survive individually.

Sunday 24th Suddenly, it is glorious and sunny. Everyone is struggling to make hay which will never be much good except to fill poor hill cows which are always expected to "rough it"; some people are even cutting grass a second time and hoping to turn it into hay.

Davy and I battled on in the garden to try and make it presentable for a drinks party which Sue and Andy are having in the garden round the lily pool. Davy cleared the worst patches of weeds and I followed, titivating and working up the ground with the three-pronged cultivator which really is a wonderful tool, leaving the ground aerated and fresh looking.

Monday 25th *Dalemain.* Clumps of *Erinus alpinus* which have seeded themselves all over the walls of the garden look well filled out. At Dalemain they have taken root

August where they were planted, so hopefully they will seed next year in all the nooks and crannies. It is is safer to plant erinus at the foot of walls and let them seed themselves into the walls; seedlings planted in walls frequently dry out and die. It is said that this plant was brought to Britain by the Romans, and it certainly grows on their forts on Hadrian's Wall where it is jealously guarded. Since planting a few well-rooted seedlings at Huntfield, they have established themselves all over the walls even into the northern side, and throughout June are a perfect picture of tiny mauvy-pink flowers. They seem to thrive in our icy winters and bitter winds, seeding and settling freely.

Tuesday 26th Many of the early summer-flowering shrubs need a good cutting back so that there is time for them to put on young growth which will be strong enough to stand the winter and to make flower buds for next season. *Kolwitzia*, known as the Beauty Bush, is spreading its lovely branches in every direction, covering too many low growing plants. Some of these elegant drooping branches draped with masses of pale pink bell-shaped flowers look perfect in tall flower arrangements with a few of the old-fashioned pink spotted turks-cap lilies as face flowers. These lilies seed themselves in the woods around the house.

On the way back from judging Fell ponies at Brough Show, I called on the Ashton Lea Garden Centre to look for long-stemmed plant labels for the stall and the selling area; fortunately they were in stock. As usual it was difficult to resist buying yet another shrub. I had seen a very beautiful apricot potentilla at Threave, the horticultural school near Castle Douglas, and to my delight there it was, Apricot Beauty, a much nicer colour than the famous Red Ace. It soon found a new home in a sunny, well-drained position half-way up the garden, beside an eye-catching berberis which produces pink and white young growth. This variety needs to be clipped back regularly to promote plenty of young growth which colours well.

Wednesday 27th Last week seeds were sown of cauliflower, All the Year Round, lettuce, All the Year Round, and a delectable crunchy variety called Buttercrunch. These were all *"through"* in about five days so the plastic covers were removed, partially at first. Sweet William, Indian Carpet, was just visible, so was left uncovered. This useful low grower fills in many dull corners and also acts as ground cover.

Thursday 28th The golden ball of the harvest moon is full, and shines brilliantly into our bedroom windows at night. How strange that the moon is such a wonderful sight at this time of year, and usually when it is so golden it means that good weather will follow.

So it was, really hot by day and one can get so much done in the garden when the weather is good. Brian is digging through the strawberries. It is no good to leave them longer in a weedy condition as it is easier to lift out the

August creeping buttercups when the soil is friable. Even if strawberry plants need to be lifted and replanted they soon settle in again.

We set fire to the dry straw before commencing digging operations. In this lovely weather it burned easily, cleaning the ground from mites and grubs and burning the dead and decaying leaves at the same time. The plants will soon recover from their cleansing ordeal and will put on tidy new growth before winter. Two rows of the oldest plants were dug out and thrown away, and runners from the youngest plants pegged down. In another six weeks these will be rooted and ready to sever from their parents to start two new rows. In addition it will be wise to buy a row of runners from fresh stock, or bring some from Huntfield where they are already twice as luxuriant as the ones at Dalemain. The cool peaty soil never fails in a droughty time of year.

The row of young plants of two late fruiting varieties look well. These were planted last autumn, Aromel and Gento and are showing a quantity of flowers already.

We were having dinner one evening in late October with our old friends Dick and Cornish Torbock, when a large bowl of beautiful strawberries in perfect condition was handed round. This was my first introduction to late fruiting varieties and we were so impressed by their flavour and quality that we resolved to grow them.

Friday 29th Plumbago is in full bloom in the greenhouse. Although it was cut well back last autumn it has already reached the top of the wall. The cuttings taken in the spring have made good plants which hopefully will flower next year. The clear blue flowers borne in whorls at the ends of the shoots are almost magical in the pureness of their colouring. Sometimes I put a vase of plumbago on a whitewashed ledge in the old part of the house, and the visitors wonder at their beauty.

Saturday 30th The greenhouse needs continual tidying up, dead leaves gathered up and long growths shortened to keep the plants bushier and a better shape. However hard one tries to carry out all one's good intentions, one never seems to catch up, especially living between two gardens and two houses.

Now that the peaches and nectarines are gathered, it is safe to fumigate overnight to rid the remaining leaves of red spider and other pests. I never feel it is safe to do this when fruit is unpicked in case they should gather any poison. Once, long ago, when we lived at Brownhill, the hydrangeas were becoming covered with greenfly. These were duly sprayed, quite forgetting that some of the spray might fall on early lettuces growing nearby. Soon after, thinking I was very clever to produce a home-grown spring salad which we ate one Sunday evening, the result was lethal and we were both very ill, Bryce particularly so as the poison temporarily affected his heart. Since then I have been *more* than careful of weedkillers and insecticides.

Ground elder, a legacy from the days when the yew branches covered the border and stretched over part of the boxwood beds, had gathered strength once more. The whole border will need taking out and digging in the autumn. Solomons' Seal and Spireas have done well but it must now have more showy plants than green hostas which were put in to fill the gaps. Shasta daisies with their clear white faces would look well, contrasting against the dark yews, and perhaps the annual cosmea planted to fill up any spaces. It is a splendid annual, strong and showy with a mass of fern-like foliage and soft-coloured saucer-like flowers; so easily grown and yet not frequently seen.

A good crop of French beans, the Prince, is beginning to gather strength. Sara, one of the girls who helps in the tearoom during the school holidays, escapes to the garden when not needed; she picked a good bowl of beans, and then deadheaded delphiniums and other plants on the terrace. Sometimes Barbara, another schoolgirl, helps too, pricking out seedlings or potting up plants into plastic containers for the garden stall. They are both a tremendous help accomplishing all sorts of useful jobs that would be otherwise neglected. Sometimes they gather the sweet peas and when there is a surplus we sell them in bunches or take them to the old folks' home where they are much appreciated. The other day, when we took some there, we were met by an old lady walking with a zimmer. Her face radiated happiness at the sight of the flowers as if one was giving her a bag of gold.

Tuesday 2nd

The terrace looks very well and full of bloom this wet season. Cut back some of the plants that have flowered which helps to conserve their strength besides tidying the border; some of the rambling roses throw up suckers regularly and it is difficult to cut them out completely when they grow as bushes along the edge of the drop wall above the Low Garden.

Wednesday 3rd

The three new H.T. Silver Jubilee roses look tremendous, planted on the old rhubarb bed where roses have never been planted before. They are now strong bushes, while two Canterbury shrub roses behind, the Yeoman and the Squire, have done equally well. Half of the original rhubarb bed remains as it always grows away early and is of such a delicious flavour and colour. Each spring, old-fashioned pottery forcing covers are put over selected plants with a good covering of manure to produce early stems. Frequently Mrs. Winskill, who has cooked and cleaned at Dalemain for many years, makes delicious rhubarb pastie, a Cumberland speciality much sought after in the Old Hall where teas and light lunches are sold. Though rhubarb has been moved to other beds, it is never as good and early as the bed near the summer-house.

Close by are some very effective plants; *Cicimifuga* or Bugwort with slender branching white spikes of somewhat fluffy florets enhanced by almost black stems, and a strong-growing silvery blue eryngium, probably the variety bourgatii. It has large blue bracts and gives a distinctive and unusual display; in front of these, an old sweet-smelling daphne and a collection of rock iris and dwarf hardy calceolaria grow – these are the miniature counterpart of what

A thousand feet above sea level *Euphorbia Griffithii* "Fireglow" and *Meconopsis grandis*, the beautiful blue Himalayan poppy, give a magnificent display. *Rosa pteracantha* with brilliant red thorns and small white flowers forms a back cloth, and (below) delphiniums, verbascums and old fashioned roses highlight the garden at Huntfield while Rosa Filipes rambles on the walls, its clusters of fragrant flowers scenting the clear hill air.

Beyond the Knott Garden where golden marjoram fills one of the boxwood beds, an ancient yew frames the view across parkland to the Ullswater fells.

Acer aureum stands sentinel in all her autumn glory in the Low Garden – Mother's Wild Garden – where carpets of daffodils and meadow flowers grow at an earlier season.

September we called Fairy Pockets, or what Nanny told the children she called Fisherman's Baskets – they have always been one of my favourite flowers.

Not knowing exactly which eryngium was in the garden, I purchased four different varieties in order to identify our own, but none of them was the same, perhaps fortunately; one of the new ones, *giganteum*, is known as Miss Wilmott's Ghost. Their blue cone-shaped flowers are set off by ghostly silver bracts, stems and leaves. Since they are biennials I must remember to collect seed; hopefully they will set seedlings themselves as these will be protected by the suckering growth of the old striped roses growing beside them.

Thursday 4th A lovely day, warm and dry, eminently suitable to collect seed. So many plants reproduce themselves more freely from ones own garden if the summer has been sufficiently warm to ripen seeds. Primulas prefer to be freshly sown, and the lovely candelabra, "Inverewe", sets seed easily. A forest of its orange-scarlet flowers make an eye-catching show. I was anxious to collect seed from the tallest of the campanulas, *Lactiflora*. This easily-grown plant with showers of lavender blue bells is one of the loveliest for herbaceous borders, but as it has tremendously deeply twisted roots it is not easy to move and requires a cool root run. One can remove young growth with a slip of root in early summer, but a batch of seedlings will amply repay the "after-care" they need to see them safely through their first winter. This period in their lives, and in the lives of all young plants, is often tricky but very necessary.

Friday 5th Took about two hundred cuttings of the old-fashioned dark blue viola *Cornutica* and set them in a frame to which had been added plenty of coarse lake sand and some peat. Hopefully they will "take" and will be used to fill two of the boxwood beds in the Knott Garden. Also set out about a hundred of the white variety which will be so pretty in a pink and silver border. At present these plants are growing among floribunda roses at Huntfield; they like the damp peaty soil and are making a splendid show at the moment. This is such a good time of year to take cutings to over-winter in a frame. Some of the various low-growing silver plants were added, and an unusual variegated mint. *Artemesia Schmidtii nana* is one of the most useful of the low-growing silver plants. Its plentiful thread-like foliage creeps outward from the centre of the plant and by the end of next summer these small cuttings will each cover quite a little area of ground. They look entirely suitable for the boxwood beds, being low-growing and tidy in their habits.

Saturday 6th Many people admire the variegated brunnera which is now fairly plentiful, planted among other low-growing plants near a spreading Victoria plum on an island, or rather peninsular bed on the lawn. This brunnera started as two plants at Huntfield a few years ago, and when split up, grew magnificent green and cream leaves; they easily revert to the parent, the common green brunnera whose lovely forget-me-not flowers on long stems are so useful for flower decoration.

Some shrubs also revert easily to the type and it is important to watch for this and remove the offending branch at once, *Eleagnus variegata* being particularly prone to revert, but these rogue branches are long-lasting in water and are very useful to back up flower vases.

Monday 8th   The high wall protecting the garden on its eastern side is invaluable for fruit trees. The wall was heightened and extended about the end of the seventeenth century, and in the archives there are vouchers for apple trees, which were planted in 1776. Some of these trees are thought to be the same ones and still give a magnificent crop of fruit. One of these trees, near the top of the garden may have been the variety listed as "Nonsuch", although when I was a child, Stuart always referred to it as "Peasgood Nonsuch" which was introduced in 1872. He used to delight in bringing enormous rosy-yellow apples off this tree into the house for the dining room. He took such pride in his fruit trees which were all pruned to perfection. This particular tree has a vast gnarled trunk and could well have been planted two hundred years ago.

One of our visitors to the garden, Mr. Choat, who lives in Epsom, close to the site of Henry VIII's palace which was excavated in recent years, was particularly interested in our ancient apple trees. It was he who kindly sought out information for me when he returned home, one of the former librarians at Epsom, John Dent, having written a book "The Quest for Nonsuch" at the time of the excavations; John Dent had been closely involved in the work.

In the fourth volume of the Journal of the R.H.S. for 1872, it relates that a first class certificate was awarded to Mr. Peasgood of Stamford, Lincolnshire, for a seedling apple named Peasgood's Nonsuch of the Blenheim Orange type. It was produced by Mrs. Peasgood from seed sown *circa* 1856. The apple is of large size (80×65mm.). Later, in the *Gardener's Magazine* for August 9th 1902, it says that Peasgood's Nonsuch was raised from a pip sown in a garden pot by Mrs. Peasgood when a child. So there is no connection between this later apple and the palace! There are a couple of interesting points, however. Henry VIII, the builder of Nonsuch, sent a Jesuit priest named Wolff, to the continent to bring back fruits and vegetables, and he brought back an apple called Nonpareil – (Nonsuch!) It is nice to think that this still healthy apple with its vast wall span is the one that Edward Hasell, known as "Blackcap", planted in 1776. Various apple trees, together with gooseberries, were purchased from a nursery in Yorkshire. There seemed to be much coming and going between Yorkshire and Cumberland during the seventeenth and eighteenth century. Possibly the road to Scotch Corner and the Great North Road was safer than the mountainous road that lay across the Shap Fells into Lancashire, although there are accounts of hunting the Dalemain hounds around Kirkby Lonsdale during the nineteenth century. Great-great grandmother's home was there, and sometimes the hounds chased their quarry into the Shap Fells, ending up the long chase near the kennels at Dalemain.

To return to the Nonsuch apple; my horticultural friend was talking to his neighbours in their garden in Epsom about the apple trees growing against their fence. Suddenly one of them said "Peasgood Nonsuch!" as she pointed to a lead label on a tree nearby; they were quite sure it was a Nonsuch with a good crop of beautiful apples, and for the last thirty years Mr. Choat had seen the tree without knowing it was the variety in which he was so interested.

An ancient greengage on our high garden wall still produces quantities of delicious fruit, and likewise its neighbouring Victoria plums. Through neglect in the aftermath of the war years these had only been flowering on their topmost branches which were resting out of reach on the stone flag coping stones. Each year of late, I have tried to "bring them down" so that the young wood can be tied in to clothe the whole wall. The greengage produced a strong shoot from near the graft, and being desperately in need of young wood, we left it hoping it was not to be a sucker. Now, after all our efforts, it is covered with small purple plums and must be removed; but it was worth waiting to see what happened.

Cauliflowers have done well lately; that good Australian variety "Canberra" is producing splendid heads. The earlier varieties grew very badly in the unseasonable drought.

Friday 12th   *Huntfield.*   The most terrible weather, gales and rain. The harvest is at a standstill. We have not even begun to combine in the Biggar area. In the shadows of the light from the front door when the dogs were put out at night the rhododendrons heaved and blew like waves in a storm at sea on a winter's night, but the most amazing sight was the mass of tropaeolum which also heaved slowly up and down on its bed of rhododendrons as if it was a mass of grey lichen or something out of a somewhat ghostly film. It was fascinating to watch as it rose and fell in the shadowy light; its flowers wasted by the ceaseless rains, but a mass of seedlings were looking well and growing fast in their bed of gravel and leaves beneath the bushes. In this cool root run they germinate freely and each year the tropaeolum weaves its red flowered net further and further across the bank of rhododendrons.

Sunday 14th   Victoria plum trees are laden with fruit. Bottled as many bottles as we had available. Oven bottling, using a sugar syrup with which to top them up is much the easiest method when one can sterilize them in the Aga cooker.

Cleaned the old dahlia border at Huntfield which is being gradually planted with modern and shrub roses, where groups of hardy agapanthus, *Anemone hepatica* and other precious plants act as undercover. The outer branches of huge beech trees overhang the border to a small extent and keep the frost partially off the plants, but the strong south west winds seem to swirl across the garden and vent the tail end of their wrath on this part of the garden. A magnificent *Hydrangea petiolaris*, some sixteen years old, covers part of the wall, while cooking apples and the unknown Brownhill rose clothe the remainder; a pretty cream and green ivy sprawls round the doorway giving colour and variation through the darkest days of winter, besides being a cosy hiding place for many little birds.

This planting should save labour and give a much longer season of colour. A wonderful display of creamy white martagon lilies multiply in coverings of leaf-mould near the Brownhill rose. These originated from one or two bulbs given to me long ago by Mary Peacock from a disused cottage garden near her home. Mary's garden at the Swaire, a picturesque cottage near the foot of a winding hill on the way to Biggar was always colourful with a chattering burn winding its way from among the woods above. Aconites from Dalemain grew in this little garden, and many other plants we had given to her in the past; now the scent of Mary's lily bulbs pervaded the whole garden at Huntfield around midsummer. An ancient thorny sweet-smelling red rose of an early tea variety was also a present, which had originally belonged to Mary's father when he was a gardener at Glamis; it too had established itself happily in our safe keeping.

Near the white martagons a planting of low-growing snowflakes provide interest before the lilies bloom. Snowflakes should be grown more frequently as they are very beautiful.

Monday 15th After the wind and rain, many rose bushes needed firming up. Some had rocked so badly that the gaps round their stems were filled with water. It is very important to give all young, and not so young, trees and shrubs "after" care attention, especially when they are tall and heavy with leaf. So a good afternoon's work was spent in this manner.

Tuesday 16th *Dalemain.* Hardy Agapanthus, the Headbourne Hybrids, are magnificent, growing into ever-larger clumps in various positions in the gardens. Tried a few plants on the terrace to see if they would withstand the possible drought, but with the rains they look well and will be better established for their second season. They really give of their best as they grow and mature.

Lettuces have grown very haphazardly this season. Sowed Buttercrunch and All the Year Round at the beginning of the month and these are coming up patchily with the sodden ground. Seeds sown indoors in propagating trays have germinated easily, as have cauliflower seed sown for transplanting in the spring.

Wednesday 17th Terrible weather, rain falling incessantly, and now gales. The heavily-laden plum trees are at risk and plums are scattered everywhere. A big branch of a Siberian crab fell – this old tree growing in the Low Garden is so tall that from the high garden one is aware of the scarlet and yellow crabs covering the branches in all their glory. Quite a big branch of the historic Grecian Silver Fir crashed on the honeysuckle fence below. The danger is that water will rot these high tears in the rough trunk and eventually kill the tree, which is a focal point at the end of the terrace.

September	Picked plums, both windfalls and others, until the long refectory kitchen table was laden. Some were sold on the plant stall, some were made into jam to be sold also, and more were bottled. The fallow deer ate the damaged fruit.
Friday 19th	Pricked out a whole frame full of Buttercrunch lettuces now nice big seedlings and easy to handle. Added more leaf-mould and sand to the frame, and scattered slug pellets before covering them with a light in the hope they will over-winter safely. All-the-Year-Round seedlings were not so plentiful, and remain in the seedpan.
'Saturday 20th	A rabbit has somehow found its way through the Deer Park wall into the kitchen garden and has eaten the French beans bare and nibbled the lettuces. A box of late sown French beans was planted in front of the tomatoes in the greenhouse with more leaf soil to bed them in; hopefully these will settle and fruit despite the cooler nights.
Sunday 21st	Dahlias are really wonderful. The big boxwood bed at the end of the Knott Garden is full of their rich colours; the plants improve and thicken with picking the flowers off for the house.

Begonia semperflorens are a picture in both gardens. Despite the effort it is to "bring them on" it is well worth the trouble. The four beds round the pool are dense cushions of flowers and at Huntfield they have done well despite the rabbits, who merely scratch the odd one out of its soil and leave it uneaten.

Tuesday 23rd	*Huntfield.* Japanese anemones are in full flower, white and pink, both doubles and singles. They like to grow undisturbed and take a year or two to make a decent clump. The pure white blooms look eye-catching at this time of year.

Wonderful berries on the trees this autumn. The crabs along the many side streets in Edinburgh are laden with fruit and the tree-like cotoneaster arching its branches over the garden door at Huntfield is a picture with the dark red berries silhouetted against the sky. Beside the tumbling burn, flowing between the house and yard, *Cotoneaster pendular's* arched branches are scarlet as holly berries. This was a cutting taken from the original tree we once bought at Ayr Show when we were showing ponies and bantams in the years gone by. Invariably we brought some new plants home from this show. Another cutting put in last autumn is ready to be moved from the frame next spring. It would be a risk to move it now at this late season.

The sky cleared out and it felt like frost, so hastily housed the large pots of agapanthus, arums and fuschias as dusk fell. Put frame lights over smaller arums and the cuttings of violas, boxes of pricked-out pinks, rock roses and others were also covered. Hopefully there will be no frost at Dalemain until I am able to make things safe before another night has passed.

September *Thursday 25th*	Up the Tweed valley the heather already looks beaten up with miserable weather. How quickly its colour has gone, and the bracken fronds are blackened and sad. The river itself is full and fast, but many of the migratory birds have long since gone south. I miss the shy willow warblers who nest and sing in the woodlands around the house at Huntfield. It is important to keep odd patches of nettles alive since these constitute shelter and nesting places for the warblers and other small birds; besides the birds, caterpillars of some of the most beautiful butterflies feed on nettles, and when young, these plants make excellent spinach into the bargain.
Saturday 27th	Wild geese fly across our fields each morning on their way to their feeding grounds on the top of the nearby hills. There they stay in the dark peaty places until late afternoon when they return to the farmlands before dusk. Little David, our grandson, who is not yet two years old, loves to watch the birds and together we follow the skeins of geese flying past. We become quite excited when yet another little party come into view, calling to each other as they steal purposely across the morning sky. Will David remember this glorious sight in the years to come, which not all children are privileged to watch, and which we take for granted. We are fortunate, for the geese, and so many other wild choruses are part of our daily life.
Monday 29th	*Dalemain.* The large pots of agapanthus still standing round the pool are unharmed, while the dahlias continue to produce more and more flowers needing to be picked regularly for the house. Tomorrow is the last day when the house and gardens are open to visitors, and I am always sad when things are quiet and there is no one to come and say "how beautiful" or to ask questions about the different plants. When one can share one's garden with people who come again and again because they enjoy its peace and quiet, and the lovely things they see, there is a point in working so hard to keep it in order. So many people live in towns, and for them it must be like a breath of Paradise to rest a little in the Knott Garden, and gaze below the sweeping branches of the Grecian Silver Fir across the undulating parkland to the fells beyond, their colours varying with the seasons, their outlines finely etched against the sky; or sometimes the eternal fells lie quiet and mysterious in gathering mists.

Let us pray that it will be possible for these precious historical gardens to be carried on by another generation of dedicated gardeners. Will another generation be prepared to work as hard as we have done? We were brought up as a wartime generation, taught to turn our hands to anything, to keep our homes and gardens going because we were certain that peace would undoubtedly return one day.

October *Thursday 2nd*	Now the visitors have gone until the spring returns, but there is activity and excitement humming, for Robert is to marry Jane Halsey on Saturday and the

house will be full to overflowing with relations and friends staying for the happy occasion. Gravel is being raked, plants are dead-headed or cut back, the greenhouse is tidied and swept clean, the courtyard looks spotless, the cobbles having been brushed yet again, and the house is full of flowers once more.

Friday 3rd I made a timetable for myself for the many things that had to be done in advance of the wedding, which made things easier to remember. We were giving a dinner party for over seventy relations and friends after the wedding and we hoped that we and the garden would be visited many times during the weekend. Large bunches of coral-coloured sedum, Autumn Joy, with its wide heads of salmon pink, were sent off to Carlisle Cathedral to be part of the decoration, for Jane being the daughter of the Bishop of the Diocese would be wed in the ancient Norman cathedral.

One of my greatest pleasures was being asked to do some of the flowers in Rose Castle, the rosy red sandstone stronghold of the Bishops of Carlisle since the days of the Conquest, and a bulwark of defence on the Debatable Lands of the Border country.

Saturday 4th The great day dawned warm and full of sunshine, the only one for several days to come. With music and trumpets sounding, Bob and his bride pledged their troth one to another.

Everything possible appertaining to the wedding was of local origin. Jane designed her own dress which was made by a lady in Thursby village, and all the flowers came from our own gardens and the moated garden of Rose Castle; berried branches were gleaned from the hedgerows. The bouquets were beautifully made by Audrey Douglas, whose husband John farms Aldby, an estate farm that lies beyond the top of the Deer Park. She even managed to find a few nerines near the summer-house which matched the bridesmaids' dresses; these were made of Liberty silk of the softest colours to blend with the flowers. Tall poles in the marquee were garlanded with berries, ivies, Michaelmas daisies, sedums, and all manner of flowers. There were pink and white primulinus gladioli, dahlias, and roses for a long-shaped vase that stood at the top of the wide oak staircase beneath the portrait of the kindly and learned prelate Edward Rainbow, who was appointed Bishop at the Restoration of Charles II. After his enthronement he restored Rose Castle which had been devastated by the Cromwellians; there were bowls of roses for the drawing room to complement its Chinese wallpaper, and posies of smaller flowers on the dining room table.

Tuesday 7th It was here, at Rose, that Edward Hasell, who bought the mediaeval and Elizabethan part of Dalemain in 1679, grew up. Being left an orphan during the Civil Wars, he was brought up by his kindly uncle, the Bishop, and his aunt Elizabeth, and as a result loved Rose dearly; they sadly had no children of their own but did much to help the children in the diocese by founding schools and scholarships. When their nephew, Edward, came to live at Dalemain, he rode the twenty miles regularly to "lie at Rose" and visit his uncle and aunt, and determined to fashion the terrace to look more like the one at his adopted home. His diary is of immense interest to our family, three hundred years later. Edward's sundial still stands on the terrace, made by Richard Whitehead of Kirkby Stephen in 1688 and the magnificent Grecian Silver Fir which he planted at the furthest end is admired by knowledgeable foresters to this day. When the good Bishop died the much loved Aunt Elizabeth lived at Dalemain for the rest of her life.

How strange and happy a coincidence that Robert and Jane should join these two beautiful and ancient houses of Cumbria once more after so long a space of time.

Wednesday 8th "Like as the heart desireth the water brooks . . . ." which had been sung so beautifully, rang in my head, and much of the other music too which had resounded through the cathedral, though one could still dream of all the beauty and holiness of the service and the pageantry over and over again.

Thursday 9th Autumn had come and soon the rains would cease; frost would steal across the ground and blanket the parkland near the river in its mysterious veil. Tender plants must be made safe, particularly some of the bedding begonias which make such excellent pot plants the following year. About ten wooden boxes were filled with these, and though they will not all survive the winter, it is worth while to attempt to save them. They were planted close together in a mixture incorporating a good deal of riddled leaf-mould and sand, and stood in the greenhouse which was still nice and airy. Some of the fuschias were potted up, but sadly only the best; one could hardly walk with ease among the many plants vying with each other for winter space. There were always wrens and robins and sometimes blackbirds following the trails of fresh earth and the possibility of worms in the shelter of the greenhouse. During the summer, spotted flycatchers and willow warblers were frequent visitors and it was so good to know they were still about.

Friday 10th Bill Lockerbie has begun to brash and thin the young trees in Lobb's Wood, mainly beeches, cherries and a few oaks which are beginning to make a fine stand. They were planted about fifteen years ago when their ancient predecessors were felled. Now, the young fretted leaves look like embroidered lace, gently moving on a summer's day, shading the visitors who love to sit on the benches along the mossy path above the beck. There they can picnic and perhaps catch a glimpse of the kingfishers who are sometimes seen, their brilliant colours flashing in the sunlight as they fly low along the water.

I gave my father various unusual trees for his eightieth birthday in 1968 since forestry was his chief delight, but sadly, he felt I was planting them for future generations and not solely for his birthday. Two of these trees, the

| October | purple form of the fern-leaved beech *Fagus rohanii*, and *Fagus zlatia*, whose leaves colour soft yellow in early summer, are growing well, while a group of grey cedars, *Atlantica glauca*, are putting on growth at the far end of the wood. Near them a few of perhaps the most graceful of conifers, the Hemlock Spruce, are growing which came from Lanrick as seedlings. They were planted in Lobb's Wood so that I will always remember the happy days with my Scottish grand-parents in the days gone by. |

| Sunday 12th | The walnuts planted between the Deer Park and the garden wall about four years ago are becoming fine young trees. Perhaps these will one day be a source of income for Robert and the Estate. The walnuts in Friars Darrock planted in the eighteenth century were allowed to grow too rough and seem to be unwanted at the moment by timber merchants. If their trunks had been straight and clean they might have helped the estate in its present hour of need. Walnuts seem to grow well on this land. Grandfather, who was a true countryman and loved the little wonders of nature, always maintained that for every tree that was cut, two should be planted. After Granny died at the end of the Great War, he continued to live at Dalemain; I loved him dearly and through him learned to love and understand the glories of the world around us and particularly the loveliness of this small corner of our earthly Paradise. We often went for little walks together to look for wild flowers and the little creatures of the hedgerows. |

Friars Darrock means the woodland walk of the friars who lived in the ancient monastery at Dacre. The brothers, in their long, rough habits, must have walked through these woods when they were probably primeval forests; one can imagine them talking to each other as they climbed up the steeper open slopes above the Deer Park and up along the rocky track through the limestone escarpments and on to the high land where they could even catch a glimpse of Ullswater. Adam Bede mentions the monastery in his writings: the friars must have fished the Dacre Beck and the River Eamont and sat on the banks above the hurrying waters which still speak of eternity.

| Monday 13th | *Huntfield.* Another horrible cold wet day after a lovely weekend. Took a number of cuttings of various shrubs at Huntfield to be rooted in sandy slit trenches at Dalemain in the hope that many of these will root to produce nice specimens to sell two years hence. The two excellent American lilacs, Bellicent and Elinor which have excelled in every way, were propagated. Tried some cuttings of a very pretty japonica, Apple Blossom, also the shrub roses Canary Bird and the Threepennybit *Rosa farreri*. This last is a great favourite, its tiny pink flowers, fern-like leaves and arching branches never fail to draw attention to themselves. Sometimes they seem to root easily and at other times the cuttings are a failure. |

October *Tuesday 14th*	*Dalemain.* There are apples everywhere and already the commodious apple house, originally the Elizabethan summer-house, is full. Usually they keep well in this airy building and last well into May. Mrs. Winskill will make many into plate tarts for the visitors teas when they return at Easter time. Blackcurrant tarts are even more delicious; there are a few recent introductions among blackcurrant bushes which are supposed to have bigger and better berries on long strings making picking easier. Ben Lomond is one of these and Ben More another, flowering later and thus escaping the frost. I must acquire some of these and keep up to date. Our own currants gave a lot of fruit this year with very little work attached.
Thursday 16th	The soil is sticky and heavy to work with the constant rain, but managed to find suitable sites in sheltered places for very precious little plants of *Anemone hepatica*, *Willow gentian* and *Gentian asclepiadea*. Forked the ground well, incorporating plenty of peat and leaf-mould. These plants were divisions of older plants lifted at Huntfield about the end of August; they were potted up so that they could grow on unchecked and form better plants. They needed fairly sunny situations where the soil would not dry out, since the hepatica flowers early and the willow gentian in the autumn, needing warmth to make the best of its arching fronds of deep blue flowers.
Friday 17th	Planted the recently-taken cuttings in slit trenches filled with lake sand, burying half their length and firming them well in. With luck, many of them will root. Nearby, the cuttings put in two years ago are now handsome shrubs, ready to be potted up next spring for the stall. These are forsythias, dogwoods, buddleias, and shrub roses of various sorts. They will all need pruning back shortly to make nicely-shaped plants.
Saturday 18th	*Huntfield.* Back at Huntfield and it was very cold with white frost in the early morning, but the sun came out and it was a beautiful autumn day. Davy dug and manured a very dirty piece of ground in preparation for raspberries. This had been planted with Jerusalem artichokes in the spring which were later ruined by rabbits. They were devoured as soon as they broke into leaf. Raspberries should be safe and are a splendid crop in this area.
Monday 20th	Eight degrees of frost at Huntfield which is horrible for this time of year. The grass will soon be valueless for the animals. In these last years we have been lucky and have had plenty of "keep" till into December before it became really cold. It was so cold I could not get warm throughout the day; by evening the frost had turned into miserable freezing wet showers.
Tuesday 21st	*Dalemain.* How quickly the weather changes in these islands. It was a lovely mild and sunny day when I reached Dalemain once more and one could not

October   have imagined that Sunday night was like winter. The greenhouses have taken no hurt though they have no heating at present; even the boxes of bedding begonias look flourishing and full of flower with a roof over their heads. Outside the dahlias, so beautiful a week ago, are sad and blackened. Even so we were able to gather the last of the damsons which are said to improve with a little frost. The best tree grows half way up the garden hill and it is noticeable that plants suffer less from frost at the top of the garden than lower down near the greenhouses. This tree was absolutely laden a short while ago, and every remaining Kilner jar was filled with fruit while the remainder were deep frozen for tarts. The last dishful from the higher branches was made into a delicious creamy sweet and a damson crumble. Some weeks ago the over-loaded branches had to be supported by strong forked pieces of wood and by posts to prevent them breaking off. So often when a branch tears off a tree the rain gets into the tear and eventually rots the tree. Later on some of these branches will be pruned back to lighten the tree, and the larger cuts painted with cuprinol or some other preparation to prevent disease entering by the cut surface. It is wise to store the unwanted props safely for another season. They are not always easy to find in a hurry.

Thursday 23rd   Once again the remains of the bedding begonias were cast away in the Knott Garden, their places taken up by forget-me-nots. The beds were forked over and a generous amount of leaf-mould scattered on the surface as well as some sharp sand. The heavy soil responds to this treatment and has improved greatly in texture.

In the old days, leaf-mould was carted in a specially-made truck which could go over the wooden bridge across the Eamont and into the great beech wood on the other side. Grandiscar provided a wonderful store of the best possible garden fertilizer. At that time an extra boy was taken on to help to collect the leaf-mould when times were hard and jobs scarce; how the garden must have benefited.

Now, under the Government's Jobs Creation Scheme, we have provided jobs on the estate for three school leavers and one of these boys has started to learn a little horticulture. His first job was to fork over these beds and later he and Brian went to the beech wood on Nutchy Hill, for leaf-mould.

Saturday 25th   The Low Garden is somewhat colourless after the bulbs have died away and the blossoming of syringas, philadelphus and laburnums is but a memory of warm early summer days, but the hum of bees in the lime trees feels warm and contented on the ear, and dragonflies poise like gossamer on the sunbeams. To add a splash of brilliance to the quieter leafier days of high summer, an old bed close to the beck was dug up and enlarged. Clumps of *Ligularia desdemona* (formerly *Senecio clivorum*) were planted. This handsome plant which grows prolifically where there is moisture and humus will give a bold effect, its deep, glossy, heart-shaped leaves always a feature with purple colouring suffusing the undersides. Tall statuesque flowers are held high on branching spikes.

October   Discovered in China at the end of the last century, this *Ligularia* and several others in the genus are most useful plants to grow. *Ligularia przewalski*, hailing from North China, is always attractive holding its wand-like almost black stems erect above its sharply-toothed foliage for many weeks in the summer. The wand-like stems are covered with countless yellow flowers, each the shape of the rare green-man orchid.

In front of the newly-planted bed of *Ligularia*, a quantity of the flame-coloured Spurge, "Fireglow" was added. This also grows prolifically in the garden and its finer foliage will complement its larger-leafed neighbour. With its wide orange-red heads in early summer it creates a marvellous show and is a plant of much consequence.

Sunday 26th   Harvest Festival, and though the seasons have been very difficult we must give thanks with all our hearts to God our Creator who never fails to give us the harvest of the fields, the gardens and the seas. The miracle happens regularly and we *expect* it to be repeated; each month of the year, each week, and usually each day, as a tiny miracle if one has eyes to see; the wonder of the corn "bre-ading" – that soft green film of tiny ears pushing their way through the fine brown tilth of lately ploughed land; tiny flower seedlings are suddenly "there!" all of varying sizes and shapes; white plum blossom unexpectedly opening on the grey lichen-covered branches of an old tree . . . and now we give thanks in the warmth of the mellow sun of an October day.

Tuesday 28th   *Huntfield*.   Every autumn the Japanese maples are a miracle in themselves. The fiery *Acer atropopureum dissectum* growing in the Wild Garden close to our kitchen door is ablaze with scarlet leaves, already dropping with the early frosts. Now, about fifteen years old, it covers a wide area. For many winters I wrapped the young tree in a tent of spruce branches until it became established, and these were not removed until the frosts were mainly past. Now it can survive our severe climate. Maples love the peaty ground, but farm manure and leaf-mould is always added; one must not neglect even established trees and bushes, since staking and feeding will make them respond a hundred fold.

Beside the maple, the old yellow azalea spreads its golden branches, the two complementing each other, and at Dalemain the pattern is being repeated in the Low Garden. The leaf-mould will find a useful home, covering the ground beneath the young azaleas planted in the last years.

The doctrine of not digging works well among herbaceous plants and shrubs where their roots run close to the surface and which feed where the sun's rays work miracles in the soil. Here, forking gently to aerate the soil does much to help, followed by well-rotted farm manure allowed to lie and wash in; ideally this should be applied in the early spring or late winter when the plants are ready to take up the food provided. It is said that lichen is a sign of poverty, but this is certainly not always true, as we well know. Leaf-mould is frequently

October more ideal than farm manure for many shrubs, and in particular for tree paeonies.

Friday 31st In the vegetable garden, digging and cleaning properly each winter is much the most satisfactory method of gardening, and whenever herbaceous plants are lifted, that piece of ground should also be well dug and improved before replanting.

The autumn gentians, *Sino ornata*, are still beautiful in spite of the cold weather, their blue trumpet flowers growing gorgeously against a background of heathers near our kitchen windows at Huntfield where they can be seen daily. Frequently the small weeds among them need to be forked out carefully and a little peat or leaf-mould or sharp sand sprinkled through their foliage to encourage them to put down more roots along their trails of greenery, each trail ending in a deep blue trumpet. Gentians "rise up" in winter time and if unattended frizzle and die in the same way that young strawberries shrivel and disappear. They are able to provide good cover for crocus and other little bulbs which are dug up so easily by the birds. Saxifrages of the Tumbling Water varieties with rosettes of silvery leaves are also excellent plants for edging a bed since they form a thick silver-grey carpet through which it would be difficult for birds to penetrate.

November
Monday 3rd Hard frost overnight at least 6°, but this time last year we had snow and miserably damp weather with it. Fortunately nothing in the greenhouses came to any harm. It is amazing how tough a lot of plants can be so long as there is no damp hanging round them overnight and they are under cover. The *Semperflorens begonias* look well, preferring a cool place on the ground to a drier shelf in the greenhouse.

Tuesday 4th *Dalemain.* Summer visitors came back to buy plants they had admired on previous visits. Phloxes are always popular and a varied collection has been built up over many years. Constant splitting of the older plants rejuvenates wondrously, otherwise the centres become hard and woody with no room to expand. It is amazing how quite small divisions in April become good plants six months later when planted in freshly-dug ground. "Silver Salmon" which has beautiful lavender pink heads is always a winner; also "Sandringham" with cyclamen-pink flowers of a great size, each floret having a darker centre. "Dodo Hanbury Forbes" is a fine pink with a red eye, but its name is so intriguing and worth growing for that alone! I wonder if some new plant called "Sylvia McCosh" will ever bloom in other people's gardens! On one occasion I thought the wide petalled pink shrub rose Lady Marguerite Hilling had produced a creamy sport only to realize later that the plant had reverted to its original form, Nevada, which if well grown, and especially against a wall, is one of the loveliest of roses. Our original plant is a marvellous sight smothering part of the house wall with a profusion of saucer-like blossoms in the early summer.

To return to phloxes, Dresden China, a soft lilac pink, must not be forgotten. At every opportunity we try to split the plants. It is better to start the summer with five small plants in a group than one huge old fellow desperately trying to expand.

Wednesday 5th   The pale pink fuschia is also admired. It is completely hardy and its name unknown. Two elderly ladies went off with their car laden with all sorts of plants and obviously delighted. I often wish that I could go to other gardens where one could buy good clumps instead of tiny and expensive seedlings.

The pale pink fuschia was one of the few treasures we found at Huntfield when we bought the estate in 1958. Its old woody growth is never cut down until quite late in the spring, when the new soft basal shoots are becoming stronger. The old woody growth provides excellent protection for primroses growing round its roots and shelter for little bulbs such as *chinodoxa* which seed and revel in the peaty soil. Cuttings root easily in a cold frame or in slit trenches in a sheltered bed and produce enormous top roots by the following autumn.

Thursday 6th   To make things easier as the years pass much too quickly, the Knott Garden must be more or less planted with permanent plants or low-growing varieties that will knit together and not distract from the little boxwood hedges which give off a delicate perfume. One of the beds on the shady side of this garden was planted today with low-growing astilbes, a rich pink variety Rheinland which I have grown at Huntfield for a long time and so was able to divide a number of plants. Astilbes enjoy rich, moist soil in partial shade, and should make a colourful corner with lovely leaf patterns and feathery plumes contrasting with the dark and formal yew hedge.

Friday 7th   Brian and I lifted the marjoram from two of the smaller beds, dividing them up before replanting in the larger circular beds which had been dug and enriched. They will form a wide circle with cotton lavender and Southernwood in their centre. The marjoram made a wonderful show during the summer, but will look more effective in their new homes with pink, mauve, and blue colours round about, besides effectively covering the celandines who have no wish to be thrown out.

Sunday 9th   *Huntfield.*   Last week we were staying at Granton-on-Spey, and while Bryce was busy shooting, a friend and I spent a wonderful afternoon in Jack Drake's nursery garden. It was like a secret garden of treasures growing amongst birch trees and maples, near a small loch. There were shaded frames full of exciting little plants for sale. A dwarf *Sorbus rectus* covered with translucent tomato-coloured berries was making an unusual show; the branches sprang from the ground like a shrub. Two of these sorbuses were soon on their way south and three varieties of dwarf spireas for future use in the Knott Garden, "Sprite", Inshriach Pink", and *Simplicifolia glaberrima saxosa*. They grow very easily and will soon multiply enough to fill one of the shady boxwood beds. A mass of dwarf rhododendrons were sheltering in an airy type of greenhouse; gentians of many varieties were still blooming though somewhat damaged by frosts and cold rains. One gets so many ideas walking round a garden like this, particularly how to propagate plants and how to protect them while they are young and need care. It is the third time I have visited this garden and it never ceases to enthrall me.

It was from Jack Drake that my original *Meconopsis grandis* came, now growing like weeds at Huntfield, and remarkably well at Dalemain.

Tuesday 11th   Struggling hard to remake the beds round the old ornamental well head in the Low Garden at Huntfield. Being very damp, the creeping buttercup grows prolifically. Davy had dug out some of the plants – primulas, iris, brunnera, rose campion, and others and they have lain nearby in the grass for some time. I reforked one of the beds, weeding carefully, and eventually replanted most of the plants – yellow and pink candelabra primulas in the lowest damp portion of this long curved bed (once part of three smaller beds), the bearded iris went in to the driest part near a hedge of Austrian briar roses. Another hedge, this one of *Rosa farreri*, the threepennybit rose, bound the upper portion of the bed, and in front, silver lamb's lug, sedums, and a frontage of catmint, this last continuing round the inside curve of the bed till it ended with an old rose of great size, Frau Dagmar Hastrup; this rose produces enormous hips each autumn which are very decorative.

Thursday 13th   Began to work on the bed in the opposite side of the well head, but it was hard work for part of this bed had been taken over by alchemila and was damper than the first bed. Nothing worthwhile is achieved without constant effort and it is not only the planting that takes time and energy but the after-care if the plants are to be worthwhile. All the above plants are found to be "rabbit proof" which is a wonderful thing to know when this part of the garden is not netted and in constant danger.

Long ago I found a mass of the alpine Lady's Mantle, growing unhampered in a Highland glen. Ever since it has multiplied prolifically, making a silvery-green mat on the edge of a little rock garden It is a well-worth plant to grow.

Friday 14th   *Dalemain.*   Planted 100 Clara Butt tulips among the forget-me-nots round the pool at Dalemain. These old-fashioned Darwin tulips make a lovely show; they were planted reasonably deeply so that they could be left undisturbed and would have the chance to multiply. Planted some parrot tulips and Mendels on the front of the house in the bed on the edge of the lawn which will first be carpeted with aconites in the early spring. Darkness comes so quickly nowadays and there is little time to accomplish very much in the garden.

Sunday 16th   Planted some extra Hyacinth bulbs in wooden boxes to be transferred at a later date to bowls for the house. Covered them with moss and left them in a dark part of the potting shed where they will remain for six weeks in order to form a proper root system. They will then stand on the staging in the tomato house which is unheated during the winter and mice will be unable to reach the bulbs. We are always catching poor mice in the seed bed where soil-warming cables make cosy quarters for the winter. These mice have such clean plump little bodies with furry coats as soft as silk, but they eat anything – the sweet pea seeds, and even little plants of *Primula senensis* which are being grown on, for the stall at Easter time.

Monday 17th   Sold a lot of herbaceous plants in the last few days, including blue poppies and Lenten hellebores. There were a few enormous clumps of the latter badly needing splitting up to be ready for spring sales. They were lined out with plenty of leaf-mould in a new selling area in the kitchen garden. This formerly difficult and very dirty corner has been well dug and divided in two with an ash path to make it easier to work. The high wall of the Deer Park shields it from the north, and the stone steps leading up to the countryside museum, now in the loft above the coach house, protects the garden from the east. Visitors can see the garden and the herd of fallow deer from this vantage point. There is plenty of room for many rows of different herbaceous plants, and cool places below the steps to root shrub rose cuttings.

I was so glad to have gardeners coming back for more plants which would help to pay the electricity bills in the greenhouse. However economical one tries to be with these wonderful blowers from Findlay Irvine of Penicuik, the bills grow larger each winter.

Tuesday 18th   Still wet weather interspersed with some lovely mornings, but the ground is very difficult to work except in herbaceous borders where the network of root systems take up all available moisture.

We cut down the long border on the terrace, removing some clumps of inferior Michaelmas daisies before doing so. It is very difficult to locate all the plants which should be removed when the border is cut, however well one thinks one knows their whereabouts. Instead of covering the border with farm manure before Christmas, we will lift and split groups of plants when the weather is suitable, digging those patches deeply and manuring at the same time. In this way, the border should look fuller and in better condition next summer without the effort of taking out a complete area of the border at one time. Old Stuart always maintained that if borders were properly manured during winter time, the plants would be able to withstand drought. Watering only brings the feeding roots to the surface when they should be searching for

November   moisture below ground. Even in the Lake District our water supply is metered, making unnecessary watering an expensive luxury.

Thursday 20th   A large patch of *Phlomis viscosa*, the Jerusalem Sage, needs dividing up. This somewhat unusual plant caused quite a degree of interest with its large, almost furry leaves, greyish in colour and yellow whorls of flowers growing in a clumpy manner. Some of this patch was transplanted to the nursery lines and some to enhance less attractive spaces in the border. It is such an easy plant to grow so long as it does not remain waterlogged.

Friday 21st   This is a good time of year to continue to put in cuttings of all manner of semi-woody plants; on the late side, perhaps, but the open weather has enabled plants to continue to mature.

Some of the shrub roses grown from cuttings needed pruning back, and part of this strong young growth was inserted into deep sand-filled trenches behind the yew hedge where they will be sheltered and not in the direct sun next summer.

Sunday 23rd   *Huntfield.*   Took cuttings of *Daphne retusa*, but these, complete with heels were inserted in a cold frame after their heels had been dipped in rooting powder. This lovely small evergreen daphne grows well behind a north wall, and scents the air for a long period. They grow on either side of the gothic-shaped wrought iron gate leading into the garden. Always cool and facing north, but sheltered by distant rhododendrons and an enormous old Himalayan cedar, they must be nearly four feet wide and half as high, drawing the honey bees to their sweet-smelling trumpet-shaped flowers in the early summer. Many cuttings have been rooted over the last years, but these must not be lifted too quickly, since they take quite a while to form a root system.

Monday 24th   *Dalemain.*   Water was pouring through the old walls built against the bank on which the high garden has evolved; it was tumbling down the steps into the Low Garden like a small river. It rushes through the wall like a fretted stream from some underground supply originating somewhere in the Deer Park. There seems to be nothing one can do about it, and when the rains cease, the "stream" dries up, but it must surely weaken the dry walls. A disused well remains half hidden by a yew tree at the foot of the steps always full of water; wherever a fortified tower was built there was need of a good supply of water. There is another well in the courtyard close to the house, and probably a third one actually in the tower, for when Willie, the Master of Works, and his assistant, Reg were doing some alterations and had lifted some of the flagstones, their tools disappeared in the depths below if they were not extremely careful! A curious phenomenon occurs to these flagstones; when the weather is to be dry the flagstones become dark in colour, and vice versa.

November
Tuesday 25th   Planted a new variegated holly, Silver Queen, in the Wild Garden where it will get shelter from the overhanging elms and copper beech trees. Hollies really like semi-woodland conditions, and the variety "Golden King" planted nearby last spring, is growing well. Hollies are such beautiful shrubs, and should be planted more widely, particularly these variegated varieties. When young they can be gnawed to death by rabbits who strip every inch of bark within reach, so it is wise to put netting firmly round them. A beautiful holly with creamy edges to the leaves, has grown on the edge of the Grove longer than I can remember. The ponies grazing in the park can reach to nibble part of its branches unfortunately, but even so, the holly has grown amazingly well in the shelter of handsome bronze-leaved maple, *Schwedleri*, and is always covered with berries at Christmas time.

A common yellow azalea, such a beautiful shrub, was planted beside two *Berberis juliana* to start a new bed where the grass had grown rough on the old river bank. Eventually more azaleas will be added, and when I am old I hope they will have covered quite an area.

Wednesday 26th   Cleaned round maples and shrubs planted in the spring, giving them a dressing of the leaf-mould lately dug up from Nutchy Hill. The Maple *Senkaki* with its coral bark, has grown well, while the very expensive *Acer Aureum* whose head was eaten by the cows in June, has one live bud. The long stem on to which it was grafted is now clothed with attractive reddish-purple deeply-cut leaves of some common variety which can grow on should the graft of the beautiful species fail to grow.

Thursday 27th   Went up to Matterdale in the evening to talk to the W.I. on the never-ending subject of gardening and plants. Betty and Margaret came with me and after driving along small-walled and hedged roads beyond Dacre we reached the small and ancient village with its stone houses sheltered by Glencoyne and the Helvelyn range; the great cascade of Aira Force tumbles down the valley nearby and disappears into the dark depths of Ullswater at the foot of the steep hill. A cosy gathering of members sat in the little hall round a big solid fuel stove for warmth The talk began with the importance of shelter in a garden and how each plant can act as a "nurse" plant to its neighbour however large or small a garden may be. We considered where each plant or bulb may grow in its wild conditions, for if this is understood, one can realise the essential needs of one's garden population. There is so much to talk about on these occasions and the additional fun of questions and discussions that time is up in a twinkling. The members much enjoyed the film taken last New Year showing something of the history of the garden and the landscaping of the parkland during the eighteenth century. We drove back along Ullswater, quiet and mysterious on this starless night, passing close to the ancient Handkerchief tree planted by old Mr. Hall at Waterside many years ago. We also passed the famous *Magnolia soulangeana* near the roadside in Watermillock, now the size of a forest tree and covered with flowers each summer.

November
Sunday 30th Hard frost and a covering of snow, but perhaps it will not last. Snow is welcome so long as the roads remain clear, for it acts like a protective blanket to the plants which are so easily harmed by frost and bitter winds. Saw a number of wrens in Friars Darrock looking for unsuspecting grubs in the rough trunks of chestnut and oak trees. In the hard winter two years ago the wren population was sadly depleted, but miraculously they have become more numerous of late.

December
Monday 1st Lovely open weather once more; how the weather varies varies from one day to another on our temperate islands.

Part of my order for shrub roses arrived and these were planted in the large square box-edged bed at the head of the Knott Garden. For many years past, this bed had been used for dahlias and annuals, but it will look much more attractive all the year round with roses of varying sizes and shapes, besides causing much less work. Catmint of a semi-dwarf variety is being planted along two sides of the roses with some low-growing mauvy-pink penstemons at intervals; these have a shrubby habit and are most attractive, and are very easy to propagate. They have been in the garden at Huntfield for many years and much admired. A good dark violet-blue erigeron grows in profusion along the front of the roses with a mass of old tulip bulbs which come up faithfully each year, well sheltered by the boxwood.

Rosa primula, the Incense Rose, was planted fairly far back in the centre of the bed. This lovely rose with small primrose-yellow flowers smothering fern-like foliage should be beautiful since most shrub roses seem to grow well at Dalemain. Its aromatic fragrance will carry in the wind.

A few of the "Canterbury" varieties of pinky-apricot colours were planted next, and Mrs. Oakley Fisher, a pale copper-coloured rose with glossy bronze foliage in the foreground – this sounds to be a rather exciting rose. Next came Jenny Duval, an old-fashioned fragrant rose of rich purple to brown and grey colouring. Little groups of tea roses, Apricot Nectar and Blessings, apricot and pale shell pink colours, were planted near the front to fill in. When the spring comes, some low-growing perennials or biennials of special merit will be grouped as ground cover. It may be a good place to plant the lovely Japanese anemones which can grow undisturbed and multiply in the spaces between the roses. The clover-pink varieties are beautiful, but the pure white anemones shine like stars on clear autumn days.

Wednesday 3rd A fairly new shrub rose, Fountain, was planted in the "Scented Garden" for blind people to give form and height to the scented lower-growing plants already there. This rose has fragrant rich red velvety flowers in clusters and singly on its upright shrubby branches – with a group of phloxes in front of it the effect should be good.

An old Gallica, *Anais segales*, first produced in 1837, was planted under the library window in the terrace border. This very fragrant rose with lilac pink flowers will again make a permanent feature in a sheltered corner.

Brian began to take out the herbaceous plants from the border under the Morello cherries. The Morellos always flower and fruit profusely and it is a race to pick the scarlet cherries before the blackbirds finish their teabreak. They needed pruning too; gradually new wood is filling the wall instead of all going to the top, however beautiful the blossom might be, peeping over the high wall into the Blind Garden on the other side.

This border has never been really clean. Mare's tail and convolvulus continue to rear their unwanted faces. The best of this border is to be well dug and manured and the rest forked whenever we notice weeds; possibly Tumbleweed could be watered on the green shoots in the spring.

I have always been loath to use weed-killers except on paths; the worm population, so important to gardeners, might become affected, besides harming other useful insects; but there are areas where one could use weed-killers and save much hard labour.

Sunday 7th   *Huntfield.*   Very cold weather again, but the greenhouses are standing up to the frost remarkably well. Boxes of cuttings covered by propagating covers look well, particularly the silver plants, which were taken somewhat late in October. There are always dead leaves and straggly ends to cut off, and it is so important to sweep the floor regularly where slugs and so forth hide.

Monday 8th   *Dalemain.*   Lovely sunny morning and in between cooking lunch for the family I began to prune the roses round the summer house and the apple trees nearby on the high garden wall. More wire and vine eyes are needed on the highest part, but in the meantime the climbing rose trees began to look more respectable. Bantry Bay, a semi-single pink rose from Sam McGredy, has always been admired by the visitors; it is a useful, colourful rose, flowering continuously for most of the season; its neighbour, Galway Bay, is even more lovely – a deep fuschia-pink with larger flowers.

The apples are very old on this wall and though some replacements among the smaller branches have grown, the old spur-pruned wood manages to produce wonderful fruit. There is always a wealth of wood to be cut back that grows above the large sandstone flags that keep the top of the wall dry. Woolly Aphis was noticed on three trees a little while ago and with methylated spirits and a hard brush we scrubbed the offending trunks and affected areas, hoping that this treatment will kill the grubs.

We must spray with winter-wash tar oil as soon as possible. The nozzle of the knapsack sprayer became clogged up after last season's efforts at spraying, but perhaps one will be located which we might borrow.

Wednesday 10th   Some new plants arrived, *Dicentra spectablis*, or bleeding hearts, which were planted in three groups on the shadier side of the high garden. Dicentras have grown well at Huntfield for some years in the north-facing border outside the walled garden, and come spring they should be split or propagated. In case this should spoil the two old clumps it seemed wiser to order a few new ones for Dalemain. One does not see these choice border plants very frequently; they produce fern-like foliage and arching sprays of heart-shaped deep pink and white flowers in early summer just when colour is needed.

Liatris, "Blazing Star", which likes a sunny situation also arrived and was planted in front of the paeonies; these lilac-purple spiky flowers open from the top downwards. Another rose, that lovely climber Spanish Beauty, again seldom seen, went into a space on the terrace wall. Its namesake has thrived at Huntfield for a long time under quite difficult conditions, so given a good start, it should be a wonderful show of apricot blossoms at the back of the herbaceous border.

It was really pleasant working at the top of the garden where one is fairly sheltered. The little groups of *Anemone hepatica* were already showing an odd blue starry flower in spite of being moved from Huntfield not very long ago, but when they were planted they were cushioned in peat and leaf-mould.

Saturday 13th   *Huntfield.*   Back at Huntfield and very wet, but Davy came in his yellow oilskins and resolutely began to cut down the borders. It is nice to get the borders cleared and dug through if possible before Christmas. Sometimes the snow has fallen on that auspicious day and on one occasion, in 1962, it was April before we saw the grass again.

Tried to replant big clumps of summer primulas in the garden round the well-head below the house. These beds were full of creeping buttercup, and have been lying half replanted for weeks. The lowest part of the beds are always wet, and primulas grow well seeding themselves regularly, but it is difficult to keep them clean.

Monday 15th   Split some of the catmint that makes an effective petticoat round the well-head and replanted them in the drier surrounding beds as an edging to the shrub roses. Only tough thorny roses that can stand up to rabbits survive in this unnetted garden. Two bushes of Roserie de l'Hay have grown into a big clump and produce enormous dark red hips. The fern-like *Rosa farreri*, the little Threepennybit rose planted as cuttings to form a hedge some years ago, has thrived. This charming thorny rose with spreading branches and fern-like leaves was introduced from Southern Kansu in China in 1915 by Reginald Farrer who was one of the most descriptive of horticultural writers. It was that great plantsman E. A. Bowles who selected the form in general cultivation, *persetosa*, from the batch of Farrer's seedlings. How grateful we should be to these persistent botanists who have brought so many treasures to our land.

Tuesday 16th   Still popping odd cuttings into sandy trenches in sheltered places where the sun will not scorch them in summer time. Whenever long strong growths of shrub roses and other shrubs need cutting back, some of these of suitable lengths are put in slit trenches and firmed up; sometimes, as in the case of the

December

Threepennybit rose, it is pieces of older-branched wood that seem to strike more readily.

Wednesday 17th

Dalemain. Two espalier trained fruit trees arrived, a greengage and a Victoria plum. Beautifully-shaped trees costing £11 each, but needing their roots soaking and a good drink for several hours before planting against the Deer Park wall in the kitchen garden. This very old and extremely high wall with big sandstone slabs along its top is part of the original walls around the courtyard. There are peepholes at suitable points through which the fallow deer can be watched, or culled. In the old days this would be done with a cross-bow.

It is worth taking trouble when planting such expensive and permanent trees. As I dug one of the holes some very old tree roots came up, proving that every inch of wall space must have been productive in the early days. Some well rotted farm manure went in, deep down, covered with soil, then the fruit trees which needed tramping firmly in, with some more manure forked loosely on top. New wires will need to be fixed to the wall behind the trees.

Friday 19th

The ancient greengage up the High Garden wall had its offending branch sawn off. I was always hoping that this new shoot which appeared when a large part of the tree died would prove to be a true fruiting branch and not a sucker. Having left it to develop for three or four years, at last it has produced small blue plums, the original stock on which the greengage was grafted possibly a hundred years ago or more. The remainder of the tree fortunately is very healthy.

Saturday 20th

Managed to locate an ancient heavy sprayer on wheels with a ten gallon tank from my sister who lives at Dacre Lodge a mile away from Dalemain. The sprayer formerly belonged to Cousin Dorothy; when I was a child she too lived at this charming old house which had been added to in the era of romanticism in the style of a Swiss chalet. Dorothy was a keen gardener and always employed a lady gardener to assist her in horicultural pursuits, while the heavy work was carried out by old Ned Richardson who lived in the village.

She and her sister Eva were born at Dalemain where they gardened happily for many years, planting many varieties of daffodils long before the turn of the century in the Low Garden and along the edge of the lawn. I wish I knew what else they planted, but their water colour paintings show the old China roses growing prolifically round the windows on the front of the house, and rambler roses trailing along the edge of the terrace as they do to this day. It was in those days that William Stuart became head gardener and lovingly continued to tend his plants until ill health and old age forced him to give up his long vigilance.

Dorothy and Eva had no brothers, and when their father died in 1910 the estate, being entailed, went to John's youngest and only surviving brother, Canon George Hasell, my grandfather. It must have been a sad day when the two sisters and their Irish mother moved to Dacre Lodge a year later, with, no doubt, quantities of plants with which to stock their new garden. In the years that followed there was much to-ing and fro-ing between the two houses, only a mile apart. My sister and I loved father's older cousins, and it was Cousin Dorothy who introduced me to the poultry world, giving me an old Rhode Island hen with her family of chickens when I was very small in order to start her little cousin off as a country girl. She gave us plants for our little gardens and we frequently played hide and seek along the river bank and in the exciting shrubberies that grew prolifically round her new home.

So it was many, many years later that Cousin Dorothy's very efficient sprayer was borrowed to spray the same fruit trees it had probably sprayed in the early days of this century. It had always been well looked after, and did an excellent job. So, weather permitting, old Joe who enjoys this sort of gardening will winter wash to his heart's content, while Brian can play "gardener's boy" and fill up the ten gallon tank. The lichens are very bad in the Low Garden and possibly a good spray may also save the old *Acer aureum* from dying back completely.

Still wonderfully open weather though constant rain makes digging impossible. But there are many other jobs to be done. When I was small there were always so many things I wanted to do, and if I was not allowed to do one thing I hated to waste time and did something else; so it is in the garden, time never waits for one to catch up, and there is always something one can manage to accomplish.

Monday 22nd   A lovely Christmas present of a pair of *Amelanchier canadensis* arrived from my sister. I had first seen this shrub, the Snowy Mespilus, growing in a friend's garden near Hutton John, its snowy white racemes smothering it with profusion, clearly visible in the dusk one evening in late May. Being hardy, one of them was planted in the windy corner near the apple house where something outstanding is needed. Its blossom should eventually be visible from the low end of this part of the garden. Growing to about three metres tall, its pink-tinged foliage which should become richly coloured in autumn, will be an added bonus to the garden.

The *Stranvesia* planted in the same area a year past is doing well. This was a birthday present from my sister and was a plant of some size when we bought each other shrubs, which we always do for anniversaries. *Stransvesias* colour well and produce an abundance of brilliant red berries. Sometimes they are clipped as hedges in Edinburgh gardens and look most attractive, especially when they are clothed with red berries in the autumn.

Wednesday 24th   *Huntfield.*   Christmas Eve at Huntfield; a mild and almost springlike day with an occasional blackbird singing the first notes of spring.

The *Viburnum fragrans*, Bodnantense Dawn, was a mass of rose-pink flowers

December   once more and since it must be twelve feet high and as broad, being sheltered by an enormous hawthorn tree and the garden wall, I dared to pick some fairly lengthy branches to put into the vases on the communion table in Libberton Kirk for the midnight carol service. With various greenery and some sprays of variegated holly from Dalemain, together with spider chrysanths as face flowers, the arrangements looked lovely, scenting the little church through the candlelit service.

Thursday 25th   Quite amazing to find the winter-flowering cherry, *prunus subhirtella autumnalis*, flowering like fairyland a thousand feet above sea level on Christmas Day. The tiny twiggy branches were wreathed in a mixture of blush-pink flowers and raindrops which hung like crystal on the tips of every little twig through which the winter light seemed to dance. There were pansies flowering, and Christmas roses pushing their buds through the ground, turning their pinky white flowers over like some little burrowing animal waking from sleep.

Suddenly it turned cold; the wind had changed and to our horror as we looked out of the door at 6 p.m. on Christmas Day there were at least three inches of snow and it was still snowing solidly – steady slanting flakes that lay quietly and firmly one upon another.

Friday 26th   Next morning was crisp and cold, the garden lay under a thick protecting blanket. No hope of Davy digging through the borders to let the frost do its work and allow us to fork out those dreadful areas of fat-hen and columbine.

Sunday 28th   The second Amelanchier was planted temporarily beside a Silver Jubilee rose – this, another welcome present from my brother-in-law which needed a good soak before it was deeply heeled in and covered with spruce branches; its buds had begun to sprout in the plastic bag in which it had arrived. But it was a fine strong bush and should take no harm. Some years ago when the ground was hard and roses arrived, they were heeled into a pile of soil in the potting shed. It was a dreadful winter and they suffered badly from not being outside. Since then plants have been "sheuched" in to a border and protected with branches at all costs, whatever the weather.

With little warning and a freezing dawn, it began to thaw by mid-day. The air changed, that lovely "fresh" smell stole across the fields as the wind arose from the south west.

Tuesday 30th   *Dalemain.*   The soil-warming cable on the bench in the greenhouse in both gardens has been switched on for the last ten days in addition to the blower at nights but the difference in the plants in these last few days is cheering. The young geraniums look cheerful, some even flowering; their top growth will make good cuttings in mid-February. The cyclamen, some young and a few old friends, are also benefiting. They have had weak doses of Sangral of late. How these plants love a little "bottom heat" to push them on, and how lucky the old gardeners were to be able to stoke their furnaces which kept themselves warm as well as benefiting their plants. Old Stuart grew wonderful plants all the year round and his dahlia tubers lay safely in boxes near the stoke hole, while ours are at risk in cold, frost-free sheds, under a blanket of dry straw.

January
Thursday 1st

There were my friends, the aconites – just a few of them – but pushing up their shining faces to welcome in the New Year. They were flowering in the shelter of the yew hedge at the end of the terrace border and a few more peeping up cautiously in other corners of the garden.

It is really much too mild weather for the time of year, and we seem to have had so many gales of late. The constant change in temperature must be disastrous to plant life. They must have wonderfully strong constitutions to survive the rigours of a northern winter.

Friday 2nd

The most terrible day of wind and rain. The Dacre Beck was almost frightening to look at from the mossy path in Lobb's Wood where one looks straight down the steep bank on to the rush of brown, hurrying water. Thank goodness the beck's course was cleared at this point and the gravel and stones piled up beneath this same bank which was gradually becoming eaten away. But even so the torrent of water may undo the good work if the rains continue.

Saturday 3rd

Huntfield. Because the weather was "open" once more Davy managed to fork over one of the borders and remove barrowloads of convolvulus roots which seem to grow worse each year, so when the remainder push their green shoots up in the spring they are in for a dose of weedkiller.

Spring *must* be on the way; aconites are blooming, much earlier than usual, and a thrush was singing despite the storms of late. There is always hope in a garden, always something beautiful round every corner, but best of all, there is peace and joy.

Another year has slipped past; another summer, followed so quickly and silently by another winter. Soon it will be spring, that ever-hurrying season, and before one realizes the time is over for sowing seeds. As each season passes, one constantly plans to achieve something more beautiful and more worth-while; better plants and vegetables where they have not grown up to expectations; but, as the swallows come and go, almost unseen in their travels – their sudden arrival and their sad departures – so the first snowdrops and periwinkles herald spring's return, making way for the tiny starry flowers of the hedgerows, the sweet-smelling tiger lilies of the woodland garden, and the colourful glories of autumn. They too are gone as the harvests of the fields are gleaned to make way for the ploughed furrows of rich brown upturned soil.

Farmers and gardeners down the ages have understood the laws of the seasons – a time to sow, and a time to reap; they have understood the urgency of those vital weeks as the days lengthen and the sun's warmth prepares the kind earth to receive and germinate seeds of every kind. Winter and the hard cold days have played their part, so that we and all the world of nature can rejoice and hope once more. Then in the quietness of the countryside, and as we walk in our gardens in the evening hush, we can give thanks to our Maker and understand a little of the beauty of His Peace.

God bless my meadowed garden
Where the fragrant wild flowers grow;
Here drifts of light-laced parsley
Shelter little plants below.

Anemones and harebells,
Star-like stone-crops on the wall;
Golden gleaming celandines
Where blossoms softly fall.

Winding waters whisper
Past the clock that tell the hour;
Marsh marigolds and speedwells
Grow amongst the cuckoo-flower.

My cultivated garden
Filled with dancing butterflies;
Rose buds and delphiniums
Reflect the changing skies.

Sunlight on the meadow-sweet;
Pearly spangled showers of rain
Reflect our prayers and praises
Which we offer yet again.

God bless these much-loved gardens
Where we plant and prune and toil.
Pray, give us understanding
Of the wonders of the soil.